Manifestation Alchemy Doctrine

Unlock Hidden Frequencies, Override Reality, and Finally
Manifest the Life They Said Was Impossible

Codex Occulto

ISBN: 979-8-89965-512-8
Imprint: Staten House

Staten House

Table of Contents

Alchemists Don't Wish—They Transmute

If you're tired of hearing "just visualize it and it will come," good. That means you're waking up.

Because deep down, you already know: that reality doesn't bend to wishes. It bends to **frequency**. To **intent**. To **transmutation**.

Manifestation isn't about closing your eyes and hoping the universe drops your dream car into your driveway. It's not a Pinterest board ritual or a morning of cute affirmations. It's **alchemy**. Raw, sacred, energetic alchemy.

True manifestation means taking what you are now—your fears, your beliefs, your identity—and running it through fire until it becomes gold. Not metaphorical gold. Actual, **tangible results**. Health. Wealth. Love. Power. Purpose.

This book is not Law of Attraction 2.0.

This is for **spiritual rebels**, **energetic architects**, and **reality hackers** who don't just want better lives—they want to **shape reality at its roots**.

Here, you're not just learning how to think positively. You're learning how to **collapse timelines**, **restructure your energetic field**, and **build an identity that magnetizes results without force**.

This isn't about "hoping." This is about **becoming the spell**.

So if you're ready to go beyond New Age clichés and step into sacred creation—let's begin. The Doctrine awaits.

PART I: THE FOUNDATION OF MANIFESTATION ALCHEMY

Chapter 1: What Is Manifestation Alchemy?

Alchemy was never just about turning lead into gold. That was the metaphor.

The real transmutation—the ancient kind—was always **about self**.

Today, we live in an era where science and spirit are no longer enemies. Quantum physics confirms what mystics whispered centuries ago: **energy responds to consciousness**. Matter follows intention. Time is fluid. Identity is flexible.

Manifestation Alchemy is the **fusion point** where these worlds meet.

It's where ancient wisdom collides with modern energetic science to create a **practical doctrine**—a way of living, creating, and becoming.

It's not a technique.

It's a **way of being**.

Manifestation Alchemy means knowing how to **take a thought**, pair it with **emotion**, infuse it with a **will**, encode it in **identity**, and act with **energetic precision**—until reality bends.

No fluff. No hoping. No waiting.

Only **embodied becoming**.

Beyond Law of Attraction: Why Doctrine Beats Law

The Law of Attraction was the doorway. The welcome mat. But it was never the full picture.

You can attract what you want all day long, but if your field is uncalibrated—if your nervous system is still wired for lack, fear, or self-doubt—then all you'll get is crumbs, not collapse-your-timeline breakthroughs.

The Law is **passive**. Doctrine is **active**.

The Law says: "Ask and you shall receive."

The Doctrine says: "**Become it—and it's already yours.**"

That's the difference. One waits. The other **transmutes**.

Manifestation Alchemy is a **doctrine** because it requires participation. It's a path of training. Integration. Realignment. You're not a passive receiver—you are the **initiator**. You don't sit back and vibe high while life happens. You step into the **center of creation** and **build from within**.

The law gives you theory.

Doctrine gives you **tools**.

You'll learn how to collapse time through intention, how to activate a magnetic field through somatic practice, and how to use symbols, frequency, and shadow to command your field like a true energetic sovereign.

The Manifestation Trinity: Thought, Emotion, Identity

Let's break it down. Manifestation isn't just "thoughts become things." That's kindergarten-level spirituality. If it were that easy, you'd already have the million-dollar bank account and soulmate on demand.

In Manifestation Alchemy, there are **three primary forces**:

- **Thought** – This is the blueprint. The architecture of the desired future.

- **Emotion** – This is the fuel. The electromagnetic current that powers the thought.

- **Identity** – This is the lock and key. The selector of timelines. The frequency you hold, no matter what you say.

Here's the hard truth:

You will **never** manifest beyond who you believe you are.

You can't think of abundance and feel unworthy.

You can't script love while vibrating fear.

You can't wear a crown if your nervous system still expects betrayal.

This is why the real work is **internal transmutation**. You're not fixing the world—you're **upgrading your field** so the world can respond accordingly.

Reality is a mirror. It doesn't lie. It reflects exactly what you **embody**, not what you hope for.

So ask yourself:

- What thought are you projecting?

- What emotion are you leaking?

- What identity are you anchoring?

In Manifestation Alchemy, we take this trinity and align it with will, clarity, and sacred structure. We don't just ask the universe. We **become the universe's echo**—with intention, with command, with resonance.

This book will guide you, step-by-step, through the seven alchemical pillars. Through shadow. Through sovereignty. Through becoming the frequency that bends the field itself.

Because **alchemy doesn't hope**.

It **initiates**.

And now, so will you.

Chapter 2: The 7 Alchemical Pillars of Reality Creation

The universe doesn't speak English. It speaks **vibration**. It responds not to your words but to your **embodied frequency**—your inner architecture. And that architecture is built on seven foundational energies. These are the **7 Alchemical Pillars**. Together, they form the invisible scaffolding of your reality.

Every result in your life—every delay, breakthrough, loop, or miracle—can be traced back to these seven elements. When one is weak, the structure wobbles. When all are aligned, manifestation becomes inevitable. Not as a hope, but as a law obeyed through energetic command.

These are not concepts to memorize. These are **forces to integrate**. You don't just understand them—you **become them**.

Vibration: The Signature of Your Being

Everything vibrates. You've heard it before—but have you ever truly grasped that your entire reality is just a **holographic echo** of your frequency?

Vibration isn't something you have—it's something you are. It's the energy you carry into every room, every thought, every desire. And here's the kicker: it never lies. You can say you're abundant, but if your vibration screams scarcity, guess what gets reflected?

The first alchemical pillar is **radical awareness of your frequency**.

This isn't about pretending to be "high vibe." It's about tuning in, moment by moment, and asking: *What am I broadcasting into the field?*

Because of that field? It's always listening.

Your vibration is your ID badge in the quantum. It tells the universe which timeline to deliver. Change the badge, change the outcome. The work begins with vibration—because no matter how powerful your will or how clear your vision is, if the frequency is fractured, the signal gets lost.

To work this pillar is to become a **tuner**—clearing static, releasing distortions, and aligning with the frequency of what you *already are*. Not want to be. *Are*.

Time: The Illusion You Must Learn to Bend

Most people are manifesting from a **linear prison**. They think in the past, present, and future. But time—true time—is non-linear. It's malleable. It's emotional. And in Manifestation Alchemy, time is not your enemy—it's your **material**.

The second alchemical pillar is understanding time as a **construct you can collapse**.

Every version of you that already has the thing you desire? It already exists. Not metaphorically. Literally. In the quantum field, timelines are not sequential—they are **simultaneous**.

So when you say, "I will have it someday," you delay the signal. You push it into a version of time where it never arrives, because *you never become the one who has it now*.

To become an alchemist is to **collapse time by collapsing identity**. You pull the future into now by embodying the emotion, vibration, and action of the version of you who already has the result.

This is not pretending. It's remembering. It's stepping into the energetic costume of your future self and walking around in it until the outer world has no choice but to keep up.

Because when your frequency says **"already done,"** time bends to your certainty.

Will: The Energetic Sword

Desire is soft. Will is sharp.

This pillar is what separates dreamers from alchemists. While the world waits for permission or signs, the alchemist **moves through the fire** with one inner command: *"So it is."*

Will is not about forcing the universe. It's about holding your energetic line **no matter what shows up**.

The third alchemical pillar is the power of **energetic dominion**—your ability to stabilize your inner field in the face of external contradiction.

Let's be real: life will test you. Not to punish you, but to ask, *Are you stable in the frequency of what you say you desire?* If your answer is "only when it's convenient," then your manifestation has no spine.

Will is what creates consistency. It's what reclaims power from circumstance. It's what lets you stay rooted in your choice, even when logic, ego, or the opinions of others try to sway you.

This is not hustle energy. This is **present with precision**. A quiet fire. A sacred no. A refusal to leak power.

Without a will, your frequency will flicker. With it, you become immovable. Magnetic. Decisive.

Belief: The Quantum Gatekeeper

Here's the truth: you don't manifest what you want. You manifest what you **believe is possible** for you.

Your beliefs form the energetic scaffolding around which your reality is built. Every limitation in your outer world reflects a belief your system holds as **truth**.

So the fourth pillar is not about blind faith—it's about **belief calibration**.

Most people are trying to manifest abundance while believing they're not worthy of receiving it. That contradiction kills signal integrity. It's like trying to send a broadcast through a tangled wire—it won't reach the field clearly, and the results will show it.

The work here is to **audit your beliefs ruthlessly**. Ask:

- What do I believe is possible for me?
- What do I believe about people who have what I want?
- What do I believe I must sacrifice to receive?

Wherever you find a belief that shrinks, dims, or contradicts your vision—it must be alchemized. Transmuted. Rewritten.

You don't just adopt new beliefs—you embody them until they're your new baseline.

Emotion: The Sacred Fire

Most manifestation teachings tell you to "control" or "override" emotions. That's nonsense. Emotions are **the juice of the manifestation engine**.

The fifth alchemical pillar is learning to **feel full and channel intentionally**.

Emotion is your charge. It's what animates your thoughts into vibration. Without emotional voltage, your desires have no magnetism.

But this isn't about chasing good vibes only. Even grief, rage, and shame—they all carry power when felt consciously and transmuted. The shadow emotions, when integrated, become **alchemy fuel**.

The goal is not emotional perfection—it's **emotional mastery**.

You learn to move energy through your system without suppression or chaos. You stop identifying with the emotion and start **riding it like a current**.

That's when your manifestations stop getting blocked by emotional resistance—and start getting supercharged by emotional momentum.

Action: The Embodied Signal

Action is where most people either overdo or underdo.

They hustle in panic or freeze in fear. But in Manifestation Alchemy, action is not about busyness. It's about **alignment**.

The sixth alchemical pillar teaches that every action carries an **energetic signature**. Two people can take the same step—send the same email, launch the same offer—and get radically different results.

Why? Because one moved from embodiment, the other from lack.

You don't act to get something. You act to **confirm who you already are**.

Alchemical action is encoded with clarity, confidence, and conviction. It's the physical exhale of an internal frequency. And when done right, it leaves a vibrational imprint that keeps working **long after the action is done**.

This is the kind of action that bends reality. Not because it was loud, but because it was **true**.

Identity: The Ultimate Architect

And finally—the core. The pillar that governs all others. **Identity**.

You will never receive what doesn't match your self-concept.

Identity is the **energetic container** of all your manifestations. It is the operating system from which you perceive, choose, act, and receive.

Most people try to "get results" while staying inside an old identity. That's like trying to stream 4K reality on a dial-up self-concept.

It doesn't work.

The seventh pillar is **identity alchemy**—the conscious process of choosing, upgrading, and stabilizing the version of you that matches the frequency of your desires.

This version already exists. Your job is to **embody her,** not create her. You align with the version of you who already lives the outcome. You study her thoughts. Her habits. Her energy. Her choices.

And then? You practice becoming her until you are **no longer pretending**.

That's when the field responds. Because you're no longer asking to manifest something new.

You're simply receiving the reflection of who you've already become.

That is Manifestation Alchemy.

That is Doctrine.

And now you know the pillars. The real work begins with **integration**. Because theory doesn't manifest. Frequency does.

Ready to transmute?

Chapter 3: The Doctrine vs. The Law

There's a fundamental misunderstanding in the manifestation world that keeps countless people spinning in circles. It's this: people confuse *law* with *power*. They assume that just because they've learned the so-called "universal laws," they're automatically equipped to bend reality.

Spoiler: they're not.

Universal laws are **truths**—unseen, unchanging forces that shape existence. But here's what nobody says out loud: **truth alone doesn't liberate you. Integration does**. Law is neutral. Doctrine is **active engagement**.

This chapter is about reclaiming that power. Because while the law may govern the rules of the game, the **doctrine is how you play—and win—it**. Doctrine is your architecture. Your strategy. Your way of interfacing with the quantum. And it changes everything.

Welcome to the moment when you stop being a reader of rules and start becoming the **author of your field**.

Law Is the Landscape—Doctrine Is the Weapon

Let's use a metaphor because this is alchemy and we love symbols.

Imagine the universal laws as the terrain of reality—the mountains, valleys, rivers, and gravity. You can't change them. They're the mechanics of the realm. But how do you move through that landscape? That's doctrine. That's your path, your method, your encoded way of navigating it.

Gravity is a law. But whether you float, run, fly, or dig underground—that depends on your chosen **doctrine of movement**.

This is where most spiritual teachings fall short. They give you maps of the terrain and say, "Here's the Law of Attraction. Here's the Law of Vibration. Good luck!" But they never hand you the tools to **move** through it with power.

Let's break it down further. Law is **passive**. It exists with or without you. It doesn't matter if you use it or not. It doesn't reward good people or punish bad ones. It simply **reflects frequency**.

Doctrine, on the other hand, is **participatory**. It's how you organize your inner world, wield your will, and craft a relationship with the field that produces results—on purpose, and with precision.

If you've been stuck saying things like, "I'm doing the affirmations," "I'm thinking positively," or "I'm visualizing every day," but your outer life still looks the same—that's because you've memorized law but never built a doctrine.

Law informs you. Doctrine **transforms you**.

The Problem with Passive Manifestation

Here's where it gets uncomfortable—but necessary.

The current mainstream version of manifestation has become a spiritual waiting room. People sit around repeating mantras and scripting journal pages like it's a cosmic ordering system. But when results don't arrive, they start questioning themselves, or worse—they start blaming the universe.

Let me be crystal clear: **the universe is not withholding anything from you**.

It's simply responding to your field. And your field is shaped by more than just your words—it's shaped by your identity, your emotions, your beliefs, and your integration. All the pillars we talked about in Chapter 2.

This is why doctrine matters. Because doctrine **activates**. It turns abstract knowledge into embodied power.

When you operate from a doctrine, you don't just ask—you **initiate**. You don't just hope—you **embody**. You don't just wait for a sign—you **become the signal**.

Passive manifestation creates dependence. It keeps you looking outside of yourself for validation, signs, or rescue.

But doctrine flips the script. It says: *I am the Source. I am the vessel. I move the field because I move myself.*

That shift? That's the moment manifestation becomes alchemy. Not wishful. Not tentative. But surgical. Inevitable.

Building a Personal Doctrine That Commands the Field

So how do you go from passive Law-abiding to active Alchemist?

You build a **personal energetic doctrine**. Think of it like your internal operating system—a mix of rituals, principles, inner agreements, and frequency anchors that govern how you show up, respond and **create**.

And let's be clear—this isn't about copying someone else's routine or mimicking a guru's morning practice. Your doctrine is **tailored to your essence**. It evolves with you. It's designed to activate your specific energetic fingerprint.

Here's how you begin building it:

1. **Claim Your Field**

   Most people walk through life as energetic sponges—absorbing the emotions, beliefs, and chaos of everyone around them. The first principle of any potent doctrine is this: *Your energy is sovereign.*

Start every day by declaring, "This is my field. I calibrate it. I command it."

 Sound woo? Maybe. But energetically, this is a massive declaration of the quantum. You're shifting from "Please respond to me" to **"I direct the signal."**

2. **Define Your Sacred Agreements**

   Your doctrine needs structure. Not rules—*codes*. These are statements of identity that anchor your being. Things like:

- "I act only from alignment."

- "I follow my highest timeline, even when logic protests."

- "I do not leak energy in exchange for validation."

These aren't just affirmations. They're your *frequency contract*. They remind your system who you are, and who you refuse to be.

3. **Create a Ritual of Energetic Reinforcement**

Doctrine is lived through **ritual**. Not in the religious sense, but in the energetic sense. Repetition creates resonance. You need daily practice—not just to "feel better," but to **reinforce your command**.

This could be breathwork, movement, journaling, visualization, energy clearing, timeline anchoring—whatever recalibrates you into the field of your chosen identity.

But the key is consistency. Doctrine without rhythm is just theory with a dreamcatcher.

4.   **Audit Your Reality With Precision**

Every result is feedback. Doctrine doesn't flinch from this—it **thrives on it**. If something isn't showing up, you ask: *Where is my signal weak? What part of me is out of alignment? What story am I still running that contradicts my field?*

This is the opposite of victimhood. It's a high-level responsibility. It's being willing to **disassemble and rewire** whenever necessary. Not from judgment, but from devotion.

Doctrine is not fixed. It's **adaptive**. It breathes with you. The more you evolve, the more refined it becomes.

And when that happens—when your doctrine becomes so natural you don't even think about it—**you become unshakable**. You walk into rooms and shift the atmosphere. You speak and people lean in. You move and reality reconfigures.

Because you're no longer trying to manifest.

You're simply **living in command**.

The Doctrine is the Key to Quantum Co-Creation

You're not here to master manifestation by following a checklist. You're here to become a **conscious participant in the dance of reality**.

The Law is always running in the background. It doesn't need your permission. But **your Doctrine? That's your interface**. That's how you take abstract energetic law and make it respond to you, personally, deliberately, and powerfully.

When you live in Doctrine:

•   You don't chase outcomes. You magnetize them through embodiment.

- You don't overthink. You trust the inner alignment signal.

- You don't collapse under doubt. You hold the field.

And most importantly—you stop outsourcing your power to "universal laws" and start writing your energetic scripture.

Because in this work, **you are the Oracle, the Architect, and the Alchemist**.

So ask yourself:

What's my doctrine?

What are the energetic codes I live by?

What rituals calibrate me?

What stories no longer belong in my field?

Write them. Refine them. Live them.

And watch how the Law—neutral, silent, ever-present—suddenly becomes your **most loyal mirror**.

Because now, you're not just aware of the rules.

You've become the one who rewrites what's possible.

Chapter 4: From Lead to Gold: Transmuting the Self First

The biggest lie in the manifestation world is that you need to change your external world to be happy, fulfilled, abundant, or free. That if you get the house, the money, the partner, the dream body—then finally, *finally*, you'll feel like enough.

But here's the raw, often uncomfortable truth: **you don't change your reality first. You change yourself—and reality follows**.

Manifestation isn't about controlling your outer world. It's about **reconfiguring the self that's observing it**. Because the observer is the projector. You don't get what you want—you get what you *are*.

This is where the real alchemy begins. This is where we stop tweaking vision boards and start transmuting identity. Where we stop scripting from the ego and start forging from the soul.

True alchemy doesn't happen in the external world. It happens in your **inner furnace**. Alchemy is an internal fire. And now it's time to step in.

The Lead: Facing the Unrefined Self

Let's talk about the lead—the dense, heavy version of you. The self is shaped by conditioning, survival, and unconscious programming. The version that learned to stay small, stay safe, stay silent. The one that whispers:

"You're not ready."

"Who do you think you are?"

"You need more proof before you act."

"It's better not to want too much."

That voice isn't evil. It was built to protect you. It's a product of trauma, culture, failure, rejection. But here's the catch: **that protective version is not designed for creation—it's designed for survival**.

And survival doesn't manifest miracles. It only manifests more survival.

So the first phase of self-transmutation is simple, but not easy: **you must face your lead**. You must get radically honest about what parts of you are no longer aligned with the life you say you want.

Where are you still hiding? Where are you still performing?

Where are you still reacting instead of creating?

Don't judge it—observe it. Because in alchemy, **lead is sacred**. It's not something to bypass. It's the starting material. The raw fuel. Without lead, there is no gold. Every trigger, every fear, every doubt is pointing to a part of you that's **ready for refinement**. No shame. Not exile. Refinement.

So the question becomes: can you sit in the heat of your becoming?

Because alchemy doesn't coddle the ego. It burns it clean.

The Crucible: Creating Inner Pressure on Purpose

You don't transmute in comfort. You transmute in the **crucible**—the intentional container where identity melts and reforms.

The crucible is the sacred pressure chamber. The energetic fire you choose to step into—not because you're broken, but because you're evolving. It's the space where you **disidentify from who you were** and stretch into who you're becoming.

Most people avoid pressure. They want transformation without discomfort. But that's not alchemy. That's fantasy. In the ancient texts, the alchemist didn't avoid fire—they **invited it**. They created the conditions for transmutation. Not just physically, but spiritually. Energetically. Emotionally.

You create your crucible through **ritual, commitment**, and **intentional friction**. Ritual is your container. It might be a morning practice, a journaling flow, or an embodiment exercise. What matters is that it happens **daily**. Because consistency is what softens the lead.

Commitment is your anchor. The vow you make to your evolution. The refusal to self-abandon when things get intense. The line you draw in the sand that says, *"I don't go*

25

backward. I don't numb out. I stay in the fire."

Friction is your forge. It's what happens when your old patterns meet your new standards. When your current behavior no longer fits the version of you that you're calling in. That discomfort? That's where the gold starts to emerge.

It's in the moment you say:

"I used to shut down when I felt insecure. Now I speak up."

"I used to self-sabotage when things got good. Now I let it in."

"I used to betray myself for connection. Now I choose integrity."

That edge, that heat, that choice? **That's the crucible.**

And you don't wait for it—you **build it**.

This is how you transmute identity. Not with lofty affirmations. With pressure. With presence. With practice. You stop being the version of you that reacts to life and start becoming the version that *restructures life* through inner command. That is sacred fire. That is the work. That is the path.

The Gold: Becoming the Calibrated Creator

Gold is not something you get. It's someone you become.

In ancient alchemy, gold represented not just purity—it represented **wholeness**. Integration. Power fused with presence. Wealth is fused with wisdom. Desire fused with divinity. And in Manifestation Alchemy, gold is the **calibrated self**. The version of you who's no longer chasing outcomes because they're already **magnetized to her field**.

Gold doesn't hustle. It **holds**. Gold doesn't prove. It **knows**.

Gold doesn't try. It **embodies**.

The golden self is the identity that holds your highest frequency *as default*. It doesn't mean you never wobble—it means you **recalibrate quickly**. It means your nervous system becomes a stable field for abundance, power, and vision.

So how do you embody the gold? You live as her before the world reflects her.

You wake up and ask:

26

How does the golden version of me move today?

What does she no longer tolerate?

Where does she say yes without overthinking?

Where does she say no without guilt?

You act not from the reality you're in—but from the one you're *birthing*.

And here's the paradox: you don't do this because you want results. You do it because you **are the result**. You do it because you've burned the lead. Sat in the crucible. Refused to run. Chosen to evolve. And in doing so, you've become the one who no longer needs to manifest.

Because **you are the manifestation.**

Your presence becomes your power. Your energy becomes your offer. And reality? It can't help but reorganize around your frequency. That's not magic. That's physics. Quantum obeys coherence. Coherence is what happens when you stop being many fragmented selves—and start becoming **one aligned source**. So if you're still trying to "get there," pause.

You're not here to chase gold. You're here to **become it**.

And now you know the path: Lead → Crucible → Gold.

Transmutation doesn't start with the world. It starts with you.

The moment you realize that—everything changes.

PART II: TRANSMUTING INNER ELEMENTS

Chapter 5: Mind Alchemy: Rewiring the Thought Matrix

The mind is not just a tool. It is an architect, a transmitter, and a gatekeeper. Every thought you think sends a signal to the field. That signal either builds your future or recycles your past. Most people are thinking thoughts they never chose. Ideas passed down, borrowed, inherited, repeated—not created. And because of that, most people are **living lives they never consciously designed**.

To practice Mind Alchemy is to take radical responsibility for the inner voice that shapes your identity, your decisions, and your frequency. This is not just "think positive" fluff. This is mental reprogramming at a soul level. It's about dissolving the invisible architecture that keeps you small and upgrading it into a matrix that matches the world you're here to build.

This is where you begin to bend your reality by first bending your thoughts.

Thoughts Are Seeds—But You're the Soil

You've probably heard the phrase "thoughts become things." It's catchy. It's true—but it's incomplete. Thoughts only become things when they are held, nourished, and **repeated** inside fertile ground.

Your mind is the soil. But here's the question: is it fertile, or is it toxic?

Most people are planting empowering thoughts in inner environments poisoned by self-doubt, guilt, shame, or unconscious programs. And then they wonder why nothing grows.

Thoughts are electric impulses. They're fast, light, and constant. But they only take root when the **identity holding them** supports their existence.

You can't just tell yourself "I am worthy" once a day while spending the rest of your time rehearsing unworthiness in the form of comparison, self-criticism, or fear.

Mind Alchemy begins by **cleaning the soil**.

That means witnessing your current thought patterns without judgment. Becoming conscious of your internal monologue—not just what you say out loud, but what you say when you're alone when you fail, when you get triggered, when no one's watching.

The unfiltered internal script? That's what's building your field.

So ask:

- What are the top five thoughts I repeat daily?

- Which of those thoughts are mine, and which are inherited?

- Which ones support the future I want to create—and which sabotage it?

You cannot change what you do not **observe**. And you cannot upgrade what you still secretly believe keeps you safe.

Thoughts don't need to be fought. They need to be **interrupted**, **examined**, and **rewritten**.

This is how the mind becomes an ally, not a prison.

Interrupting the Default: Pattern Breaks and Thought Loops

Once you become aware of your thoughts, the next step is to **interrupt the loops** that keep you spinning in old realities.

Your brain is a pattern recognition machine. It loves efficiency. It will always default to the most familiar thought, even if that thought hurts you—because familiarity, to the brain, equals safety.

That's why you keep thinking, "I'll never figure it out," even after all your growth. Or why do you still expect disappointment after a win? It's not because you're broken—it's because your brain is addicted to what's *known*.

Mind Alchemy breaks this cycle.

To rewire the thought matrix, you must disrupt the familiar and create **new neural grooves**. Here's how:

1. **Catch the Loop in Real-Time**

   The moment you hear yourself rehearsing a familiar negative thought—pause.

Don't judge it. Don't push it away. Just label it. "Oh, that's the 'I'll fail anyway' script again." Naming it reduces its power. You become the observer, not the prisoner.

2.   **Insert a New Command**

The brain needs replacement, not just removal. You don't just stop thinking about something—you replace it with a higher truth.

"This doesn't align with who I'm becoming. Let me choose again."

Repetition here is crucial. The more you say it, the more the mind begins to accept it as the new normal.

3.   **Anchor It in the Body**

Thoughts don't live in the mind alone. They echo in your body. So when you shift a thought, shift your posture, your breath, your movement.

Standing taller while thinking "I am powerful" encodes it deeper than just repeating it while slouched over and shallow breathing.

Embodied thinking becomes **vibrational thinking**.

Over time, these micro-interruptions create a macro-shift. The default wiring breaks down, and the new matrix begins to build. You're no longer thinking old thoughts with a new language—you're thinking **new thoughts with a new embodiment**.

That's the difference between mental tricks and mental transformation.

Designing the Inner Voice of the Future Self

Now that you've interrupted the old and cleaned the soil, it's time to consciously **design the thought architecture** of your future self.

This is the most overlooked part of manifestation work—yet it's one of the most powerful. Your future reality requires a different voice in your head. A different narrative. A different relationship to challenge, to risk, to worthiness.

If your current thoughts are shaped by your past, your new thoughts must be shaped by your **next-level identity**.

Here's how you begin crafting that voice:

1. **Create a Thought Inventory for the Next Version of You**

Close your eyes. Tune in to the version of you who already lives your desired reality. Maybe she's running a successful business. Maybe he's deeply in love. Maybe they're leading, thriving, overflowing.

Now ask:

What do they think on a normal Tuesday morning?

What do they tell themselves when they make mistakes?

What do they believe about receiving, giving, leading, and resting?

Write these thoughts down. Turn them into a daily playlist. Not affirmations that feel fake. But **beliefs that stretch you toward embodiment**.

2. **Speak from the Future, Not to I**

Stop begging the universe for change. Start **thinking as if you are the universe's partner in creation**.

Your inner voice should speak with authority, not desperation. With certainty, not begging.

"I'm preparing the space for it—it's already mine."

"I'm calibrating to the frequency where this is obvious."

"I trust the delay because I trust my development."

These aren't delusions. These are commands. And the field listens to **command energy**.

3. **Repeat Until It Feels Like Home**

Repetition isn't boring—it's rewiring. The more you repeat a thought that aligns with your future self, the more it becomes automatic. And when it becomes automatic, it becomes your **default vibration**.

When your dominant thoughts match your dominant desires, the universe doesn't resist—it **delivers**.

So if you want to collapse timelines, start here. Start with the thoughts you think when no one is watching. That's the code that sets your quantum address.

32

The future isn't something you find. It's something you **remember and embody—one upgraded thought at a time**.

Final Words on Mental Alchemy

Mind Alchemy is not a one-time hack. It's not about perfect thoughts or flawless mantras. It's about **becoming the source of your mental frequency**. Choosing thoughts that match your power—not your past. Creating a mind that holds the signal—not breaks it.

When you master the thought matrix, you stop trying to "think your way into results."

You start letting your thoughts become **vibrational software**—running in the background, tuning your field, speaking to the quantum in real-time.

You are not your thoughts.

But you are the one who trains them, chooses them, and uses them to build the world around you.

Thoughts are not just tools.

They are **spells**.

And you, Alchemist, are learning to cast with precision.

Chapter 6: Emotion Alchemy: Feel It to Forge It

If thoughts are the blueprint, then emotions are the flame that forges the design into form. They are not obstacles. They are not messes to clean up. Emotions are raw energetic currency, and in the alchemist's hands, they become the most powerful fuel for transformation.

This chapter is not about feeling good all the time. That's a myth for amateurs. This is about feeling **full**, feeling **conscious**, and feeling with **intentional direction**. When you learn to work with your emotional body instead of against it, you stop leaking energy and start generating magnetism.

Emotion Alchemy is the art of recognizing every feeling—not just joy, but grief, rage, doubt, and shame—as a potent ingredient in your manifestation spell. And when you stop labeling emotions as "bad" or "wrong," you gain access to the full spectrum of your power.

It's time to turn your heart into a forge.

Emotion is Energy in Motion—But Only if You Let It Move

Emotion is not mental. It's **somatic**. It lives in the body. It vibrates, pulses, and communicates long before your mind catches up. The word "emotion" itself means *energy in motion*. But for most people, that motion gets blocked, judged, or suppressed.

The result? Emotional congestion. Static in the field. A body is full of trapped frequencies sending out contradictory signals.

You say you want expansion, but your chest is clenched with fear.

You script abundance, but your belly is twisted with unworthiness.

You meditate on love, but your heart still aches with resentment.

And so the field responds with mixed results.

The first step of Emotion Alchemy is **permission**. You must allow yourself to feel everything. Not just the pretty feelings. Especially the ones that scare you. Why? Because suppressed emotion doesn't disappear. It **manifests sideways**—as sabotage, indecision, fatigue, distraction, and overthinking.

There is no bypass here. You have to let the energy move. Fully. Safely. Consciously.

How? Through **embodiment practices**, **breath**, **sound**, **movement**, and **awareness without judgment**.

When you let sadness move, it softens into clarity.
 When you let anger move, it sharpens into the boundary.
 When you let joy move, it amplifies into magnetism.

Emotion is a sacred signal. But only if you let it complete its cycle.

So next time you feel something intense—pause. Don't fix it. Don't label it. Don't rush it away with a mantra or a scroll on Instagram. Ask:

Where is this emotion in my body?
 What does it want me to hear, honor, release, or reclaim?

Then breathe into it. Move with it. Let it rise. Let it pass. Let it teach.

Because emotion that's felt fully becomes **alchemy**.

Your Emotional Signature Is Your Magnetic Field

The quantum field doesn't respond to what you think you want. It responds to the **emotional frequency you hold most consistently**.

Your emotional state is your broadcast. Your signature. Your energetic fingerprint. And it is far more potent than any vision board you could tape to your wall.

Here's the kicker: it doesn't have to be a constant joy. That's not real, and it's not sustainable. What the field responds to is **emotional congruence**—feeling what is real, processing it, and returning to coherence.

Congruence means emotional honesty. Not fake positivity.
 Coherence means energetic stability. Not denial of feeling.

When you are emotionally congruent, your nervous system relaxes. Your field clears.

Your manifestation signal becomes **sharp, clean, and direct**.

That's when you stop chasing outcomes and start attracting them.

So the question is not "How do I feel good all the time?"

The real question is "What emotional signature do I want to stabilize in my field—and what do I need to feel and clear to hold it?"

Let's say you want to stabilize **abundance**. That's not just a mindset—it's a felt frequency. It has a shape. A tempo. A weight. What does abundance feel like in your body? Spacious? Steady? Radiant? Rooted?

Now contrast that with the emotional signatures of lack: anxious, tight, restless, desperate.

If your body is still rehearsing lack, it will override your affirmations every time.

Emotion Alchemy is how you train your body to **default to the frequency you want to manifest from**. This is deeper than thought. It's about nervous system attunement.

You do this by building **emotional muscle memory**. That means:

- Practicing the felt sense of safety, joy, and power—even without a trigger.

- Identifying emotional leaks (jealousy, guilt, shame) and cutting the source.

- Building rituals that flood your system with chosen frequencies.

Over time, your emotional setpoint rises. And as it rises, your field magnetizes experiences that match it—not because you tried harder, but because you're simply **a vibrational match**.

That's magnetism. Not from pushing. From **holding**.

Feelings as Fuel: Using Emotion to Forge Desire Into Form

There's a hidden reason your manifestations might feel flat, distant, or slow. And it's this: **you're not emotionally invested enough**.

Desire without emotion is just an idea. But desire fused with **charged feeling** becomes a living frequency. That's what reaches the quantum and collapses timelines.

Emotion is the *activator*. It's what takes your intention and infuses it with voltage.

Think about it: when did you create the most change in your life? Probably when you were emotionally lit—on fire with purpose, frustrated enough to move, heartbroken enough to shift, excited enough to leap. That wasn't a weakness. That was **raw fuel**.

Emotion isn't the enemy. It's the engine.

So here's how to use it like an alchemist:

1.   **Feel the Desire in the Body, Not Just the Mind**

You don't just want a result. You want the **feeling** that the result promises. So skip the outer goal and drop into the emotion behind it.

What does it feel like to live in overflow?

What does it feel like to be chosen, respected, or seen?

What does it feel like to walk through life with quiet, unwavering power?

Now breathe into that. Amplify it. Stay there. Not to escape reality—but to **encode a new one**.

2.   **Use Emotional Contrast to Trigger the Shift**

When you notice emotions you don't want—jealousy, fear, sadness—don't resist them. Use them. Ask:

What does this feeling show me about what I deeply care about?

What new choice is this emotion inviting me to make?

Contrast is clarity. If something hurts, it's showing you where your alignment has cracked. Not to punish you—but to **wake you**.

3.   **Anchor the Emotion Into Action**

Emotion alone isn't enough. It must be expressed through **energetic action**. That might mean making a bold decision, speaking a boundary, dancing it out, or creating something from the frequency you just accessed.

The feeling is the spark. But **embodied action** is what forges it into form.

That's how you transmute emotion into the material.

You don't just feel to feel.

You feel to fuel the field.

Emotion is not a weakness. Emotion is **power in motion**.

When you master it, you master **momentum**.

Final Words on Feeling Like an Alchemist

To be an alchemist is to **stop fearing your feelings**.

It is to understand that emotion isn't something to control or avoid—it's something to harness, direct, and honor.

Emotion tells you what's true. Emotion points to what matters. Emotion carries the code of your next transformation. And when you learn to work with it instead of shaming it, you become emotionally sovereign.

You become a clean channel. A magnetic field. A forge.

No longer chasing a high, but holding the **sacred heat** of your evolution.

Let your feelings move you.

Let them wake you up.

Let them reshape the field.

Because in the hands of an alchemist, emotion becomes **gold**.

Chapter 7: Body as Cauldron: The Energetic Container

You can think the thoughts. You can feel the feelings. But until your body holds the frequency, nothing truly sticks. This is the part no one tells you. Manifestation doesn't live in your vision board. It lives in your **nervous system**. In your **posture**. In your **breath, habits, movement, stillness, presence**.

Your body is not just your vehicle. It is the **cauldron**. The place where energy gets concentrated, transmuted, and amplified. If your body can't hold the frequency of your desire, that desire will either float in the field unanchored—or worse, be rejected by your system because it feels *unsafe*.

This chapter is not about physical health—though that matters. It's about **energetic capacity**. About embodiment. About making your body a match for the life you say you want. Because if you want to be magnetic, abundant, intuitive, powerful—you can't just think like it. You have to *move* like it. *Stand* like it. *Breathe* like it.

Your body is where the spell becomes real. And the cauldron must be clean, stable, and sacred.

The Nervous System is the Frequency Gatekeeper

Let's begin with the foundation: your nervous system. This is the gatekeeper of your manifestation. The bridge between your conscious desires and your unconscious readiness.

You may think you're ready for success, love, money, and visibility. But if your nervous system perceives those things as threats, it will **block, distort, or delay** them.

That's not sabotage. That's protection.

The body always prioritizes *safety* over *expansion*. If a new reality feels destabilizing—even if it's what you want—your body will unconsciously revert to the familiar. That's why people go back to old relationships, shrink after big wins, or freeze when opportunity knocks.

40

So the first level of body alchemy is **nervous system regulation**. You must teach your body that expansion is safe. That power is safe. That receiving is safe.

You do this through daily practices that calm and strengthen your system's capacity to hold more energy:

- **Breathwork** to move energy and release stored stress.

- **Cold exposure or heat therapy** to train response under intensity.

- **Grounding practices** (barefoot contact with the earth, presence-based movement) to reorient to the now.

- **Somatic awareness** to track sensation and release contraction.

The goal is not to "be calm all the time." The goal is to build **range**. To feel more, hold more, process more—*without collapse*.

A regulated nervous system becomes a stable signal. It stops flinching from power. It stops rejecting goodness. It starts trusting expansion.

And that trust? That's what tells the quantum field: *we're ready now.*

Because the field responds not to what you say—but to what your body *believes is safe to receive.*

Movement as Magnetic Ritual

The way you move tells a story. It communicates not just who you are, but **who you believe yourself to be**. Alchemists understand this. They know that movement is not random—it's encoded.

A slouched posture says, "I shrink. I protect. I brace."
 An upright, open posture says, "I receive. I lead. I allow."

The way you walk into a room shifts your electromagnetic field. The way you hold your shoulders changes your breath pattern. The way you sit tells your nervous system how to prepare.

That's not just physiology. That's **energetic broadcasting**.

So the second level of body alchemy is to **move like your next self**. Not in

41

performance—but in *practice*. In rehearsal. In embodiment.

Ask yourself:

- How does the future version of me walk into the world?

- How do they sit, stand, move through conflict, and enter conversations?

- How do they breathe when they speak?

Then start *doing that*. Not someday—*now*.

This doesn't mean faking confidence. It means creating micro-adjustments that **signal your evolution in motion**.

Try this:

- Wake up and move through your day as if you're already holding the result you desire. See how your posture shifts. Your tone. Your pacing.

- Use embodiment practices like intuitive dance, yoga, martial arts, or flow movement—not as workouts, but as **energetic attunement sessions**.

- Speak from your belly, not your throat. Let your words drop into your body and rise from it. That's how you *become the message*.

Your body remembers what your mind forgets. Train it. Honor it. Trust it.

Because the way you move becomes the way you **manifest**.

Rituals to Anchor Frequency in the Flesh

Words are air. Emotion is current. But **ritual** is what crystallizes energy into habit. The body responds to the **pattern**. It loves rhythm, repetition, and ritual. This means you can train it to *expect* alignment—just like you can train it to expect anxiety or chaos.

The third level of body alchemy is about creating daily, intentional rituals that **anchor your desired frequency into the flesh**.

These rituals don't have to be elaborate. The more *doable*, the more *effective*. The point is consistency. Repetition creates embodiment.

Here are a few to start with:

1. Morning Frequency Activation

Before checking your phone, give your body a moment to tune in.

Ask: What frequency do I choose to carry today? Confidence? Clarity? Devotion?

Then embody it. Move with it. Breathe it in. Speak one sentence aloud that claims it.

This five-minute ritual sets your nervous system up for *deliberate coherence*.

2. Receiving Practice

Lie down. Place your hands on your heart and belly. Say out loud: "It is safe to receive."

Then breathe deeply and imagine your body opening like a vessel.

Notice what parts clench or resist. That's your work. Do this daily until it becomes easy.

Manifestation isn't just about sending signals—it's about becoming **receptive to response**.

3. Embodied Decision-Making

Every time you're faced with a choice, ask your body:

Does this feel like contraction or expansion?

Does this align with the identity I'm becoming?

Feel the signal. Then act from that—not from fear, logic, or habit.

This trains your body to **lead your reality**, not just survive it.

When your rituals become sacred instead of robotic, your body becomes **a sanctuary for transformation**. Not just a tool—but a temple.

You stop treating your body like an inconvenience and start treating it like the most **reliable portal** to reality creation.

Final Words on Becoming the Vessel

Your body is not just along for the ride—it *is* the ride.

It is the translator between your soul's command and the physical world's response. It's where belief becomes behavior. Where emotion becomes expression. Where frequency becomes a force.

If your body isn't on board with your manifestation, it will quietly override it. If your body isn't safe with expansion, it will shrink. If your body doesn't trust your vision, it won't anchor it.

This is why so many spiritual seekers stay stuck: they do all the mindset work, all the inner child healing, all the journaling—and wonder why they still can't seem to receive.

It's because their **bodies never got the memo**.

You're not here to float away into bliss. You're here to **ground heaven into form**.

And that requires a body that can hold more light, more energy, more responsibility, more visibility, more *you*.

You are the cauldron.

Keep it strong.

Keep it sacred.

Keep it alive.

Chapter 8: Desire as Divine Blueprint

Desire has been misunderstood, shamed, and misused for centuries. In some spiritual circles, it's labeled egoic. In others, indulgent. In the productivity-driven world, it's commodified and manipulated. But in alchemy, desire is none of those things.

Desire is a **divine blueprint**. A signal. A summons. A form of intelligence that speaks not to your ego, but to your essence.

You don't desire something because you're greedy broken or bored. You desire it because a part of you—your soul, your highest self, your energetic core—**knows it's meant for you**.

And not only meant for you but available. If it wasn't possible, the desire wouldn't arrive. Desire is *proof of permission*.

This chapter is an invitation to stop second-guessing your wants and start honoring them as sacred. Because your future isn't built through discipline alone. It's guided by the **fires of authentic longing**.

When the desire is embodied, clarified, and followed—it becomes destiny.

Desire is the Language of the Soul

Desire is not a product of lack. It's a **creative impulse**. A soul-level whisper saying, "There's more available to you—go get it." But we're taught early to distrust that voice. To tone it down. To make our dreams more realistic. To justify them with logic.

So we start wanting what's safe instead of what's true.

We shrink our dreams into checklists.

We suppress the fire and then wonder why we feel stuck.

Let me be clear: not every craving is sacred. Not every impulse is intuitive. But pure, soul-anchored desire? That is not emotional noise. That is **a compass**. That's how your higher self communicates direction.

You must learn to tell the difference between:

- Egoic desire (driven by comparison, fear, validation).

- Suppressed desire (quieted by shame, guilt, trauma).

- True desire (rooted in essence, aligned with your highest timeline).

True desire feels clean. Quiet, sometimes. But persistent. It lives in your belly, not just your mind. It energizes rather than depletes. And when you listen to it, life opens.

To access it, you must silence the noise.

That means clearing the opinions, the filters, and the inherited rules about what's "too much" or "not realistic." It means sitting in stillness and asking, *If no one judged me, what would I allow myself to want?*

Then you listen—not for the loudest voice, but the **truest one**.

This is how the alchemist chooses their path—not by logic, but by inner fire.

Purifying Desire: From Conditioning to Clarity

Desire, in its rawest form, is sacred. But often what we think we want has been distorted by **conditioning**. We've been programmed by media, marketing, family, religion, and social norms to want what others value—not what our soul came here for.

So before you build your life around a desire, you must ask: *Is this mine? Or is this a performance I've inherited?*

Purifying desire is the process of clearing the static and letting the authentic signal come through.

Here's how you begin:

1.   **Audit Your Core Desires**

Write down your biggest wants. Wealth. Partnership. Visibility. Impact. Now go deeper. For each one, ask:

- Where did this desire originate?

- When did I first decide I wanted this?

- Do I still want it, or is it a habit?

- Who benefits from me pursuing this?

Sometimes you'll realize that what you've been chasing is a borrowed dream. That's not failure. That's **freedom**. You get to release it and make room for something truer.

2.   **Trace the Emotional Thread**

Every true desire carries an emotional signature. It's not about the object—it's about the *feeling it unlocks*. Trace your desire back to the emotion beneath it.

Do you want money—or do you want freedom, safety, play?

Do you want recognition—or do you want to feel seen, heard, or affirmed?

When you know the feeling you're after, you can find **more aligned paths** to it. Sometimes your soul wants to teach you how to embody the feeling *before* the form arrives.

This is not settling. This is preparing your frequency to **receive the match**.

3.   **Let Desire Evolve**

Your wants will change as you grow. Let them. What served your past self may not serve your next self. And if a desire is dying, it doesn't mean you're failing. It means your blueprint is **updating**.

Don't cling to expired dreams just because you've invested time in them. Alchemy requires fluidity. Identity must be able to stretch. Desires must be able to die and resurrect.

If you keep honoring what no longer fits, you block what *does*.

Let your longings evolve. They're your soul's way of guiding you through different chapters of embodiment.

That's not confusing. That's **cosmic clarity**.

Desire as Directive: Turning Longing Into Strategy

Desire becomes powerful when it's no longer abstract. When it's **translated into action**. This is where most people fall short—they dream, they visualize, they affirm… but they never move.

Desire without direction becomes stagnation. A burning that eats instead of fuels.

So the next step in Emotion Alchemy is to **treat desire like divine instruction**. It's not a hint. It's a command.

Ask: *If this desire is sacred, what is it asking me to do right now?*

Here's how you work with it strategically:

1.   **Make Your Desire Tactical**

Take your desire and turn it into steps. Not as a to-do list from the ego, but as a roadmap from the soul.

If you desire to lead, ask: Where can I speak? What can I teach now, imperfectly?

If you desire to love deeply, ask: What part of me needs to open more to give and receive that?

If your desire is prosperity, ask: How can I embody abundance before the money lands?

Desire is not passive. It wants your **participation**.

2.   **Let the Desire Restructure You**

Your desire is not just something to chase. It's something to *become worthy of.* Not in the sense of being "enough," but in the sense of being *aligned.*

If your desire is expansion, it will ask you to let go of contraction.

If your desire is visibility, it will ask you to heal your fear of being seen.

If your desire is power, it will ask you to stop hiding behind indecision.

This is what alchemists do: they let desire transform them into the person who naturally attracts the thing.

Desire becomes the **furnace of refinement**.

3.   **Act Before You're Ready**

You won't feel ready. That's the point. Desire often comes before capacity—but only so you'll *build the capacity by acting.*

The quantum field rewards courage, not hesitation. The second you start moving in the direction of your desire—even clumsily—you shift timelines.

Because you're no longer dreaming. You're **signaling readiness**.

And that signal? That's what the field responds to.

Desire wants to move through you.

Desire wants to shape you.

Desire wants to *use* you.

Let it.

Final Words on the Sacred Fire

Desire is not frivolous. It's not greedy. It's not random.

It is **coded instruction**. Blueprint. Invitation. Portal. It's your higher self handing you the map to your next initiation.

When you ignore it, life feels flat. When you obey it, life becomes electric.

You don't have to justify what you want. You just have to be honest about it. Hold it with reverence. Move with it. Let it undo the parts of you that are too small to hold it—so that what remains is pure, powerful, and *ready*.

Your desires are sacred.

They are not here to tease you.

They are here to **transform you**.

Now it's time to put it all into practice.

PART III: THE SACRED PRACTICE

Chapter 9: The Daily Alchemy Ritual

Manifestation isn't a one-time visualization or a once-a-month moon ritual. It's a daily embodiment. A consistent decision to live, move, and think from your chosen frequency—even when external results haven't caught up yet. Especially then.

This is what most people miss. They try to "do the manifestation thing" once in a while, and wonder why it doesn't stick. But frequency doesn't care what you think once a week. It responds to your **dominant energy**. And dominant energy is built through **ritual**.

Alchemy isn't chaotic. It's precise. It's structured. There is a method to the magic. And that method starts with how you **start your day**, **move through it**, and **close it with intention**.

A daily alchemy ritual isn't about being perfect—it's about building a field. A magnetic atmosphere around you signals to the quantum, *"I am already the version of me who receives this."* When you do that consistently, the field has no choice but to mirror it.

This chapter is about building that ritual. Not a generic one. **Yours**. One that works with your energy, your life, and your desired reality. We'll break it down step-by-step so it becomes not just a practice, but a lifestyle. A rhythm that bends reality.

Morning: Claiming Frequency Before the World Claims You

Your morning is your most powerful portal. Before your mind remembers who you were yesterday, before you check your phone and download everyone else's energy—there is a tiny window where your field is **malleable**. This is where alchemists make moves.

The purpose of the morning ritual is not productivity—it's **possession of frequency**. You're not trying to get more done. You're trying to start the day already aligned with who you're becoming.

Start with stillness. Even just sixty seconds. Sit or lie down and ask yourself: *What frequency do I choose to carry today?*

Not a to-do list. A to-be list.

Powerful. Receptive. Clear. Devoted. Magnetic.

Pick one. Then breathe into it.

Now **anchor it in your body**. Through breath, movement, or sound. Stretch with intention. Place your hand on your chest and say your chosen frequency out loud. Walk to the kitchen as that version of you. Make your coffee as them. Feel your spine adjust, your breath deepens, and your energy clicks in.

Even if it's five minutes—do it. Not to "feel good" but to **claim energetic authorship** of your day.

Optional tools to include:

- Journaling: "Here's who I am today. Here's what I'm calibrating to."

- Mirror work: Eye contact with self while affirming truth.

- Visualization: Not fantasy, but *felt presence*. Embody it now.

- Breathwork: Three deep, conscious breaths while repeating your chosen state.

The morning isn't about fixing anything. It's about *remembering*. You're not becoming magnetic—you're **returning to it**.

And when you start the day from there, the world shifts in response.

Midday: Holding the Field When Life Gets Loud

The real alchemy isn't in the quiet morning—it's in how you *hold your frequency when chaos kicks in*. Because manifestation doesn't happen in your sacred corner. It happens in traffic. In meetings. In your inbox. In life.

The purpose of your midday ritual is **recalibration**. A check-in. A reset button for your field. This is where you remember that even in motion, even in stress—you are still the alchemist.

This doesn't have to be long or dramatic. It's about **micro-moments of energetic ownership**.

Try this:

- Pause mid-morning and mid-afternoon for 60 seconds. Breathe. Tune in. Ask: *What frequency am I leaking right now? What frequency do I choose instead?*

- Set a phone alarm that says "Remember who you are." Let it break the autopilot.

- When triggered, take a sacred pause. Drop into your body. Even one conscious breath is a shift.

- Speak your field into coherence: "I return to calm." "I return to clarity." "I choose overflow."

You are not a victim of your day. You are **the architect of how you move through it**.

Move a ritual too. Walking isn't just getting from A to B—it's a chance to realign your energy. Your pace, your posture, your presence—all of it sends signals. Walk like your field is turned on. Like your desires are in progress. Like you are *already it*.

Midday alchemy is about **maintenance**. You don't let your energy run wild. You groom it. You tend to it. You **curate your frequency** like it's a sacred space—because it is.

This is how you become unshakeable. Not by avoiding life—but by mastering your presence *in the middle of it*.

Evening: Locking in the Signal Before You Sleep

Nighttime is when your body rests—but your field is *wide open*. Your subconscious is more active. Your dreams are portals. This is why how you close your day matters just as much as how you start it.

Most people end their night in unconscious consumption. Scrolling, zoning out, collapsing into bed with no intentional closure. But an alchemist knows better.

Your **evening ritual** is about two things: **integration and encoding**. You integrate what the day offers, and you encode what you're becoming.

Here's a simple, powerful sequence:

1. **Reflect without judgment**

Ask: *What did I calibrate to today? What moments pulled me out of my chosen field? Where did I surprise myself? Where did I move like my next-level self?*

This is not for guilt. It's for *awareness*. You can't shift what you don't track.

2.   **Celebrate the evidence**

Even tiny wins. A moment of confidence. A no-spoken with clarity. A bold decision.

The more you celebrate alignment, the more your nervous system *learns to stabilize it.*

3.   **Speak your future into the dark.**

Before sleep, affirm not as a chant—but as a command.

"I am the one who holds the field."

"I let go of what no longer serves."

"I trust what's unfolding."

"I am already the version I've been calling in."

Speak it. Whisper it. Let it sink.

4.   **Visualize one scene**

Not ten. Just one. A felt, embodied moment from your desired reality. A conversation. A morning. A sensation. Breathe into it as you drift. Let it program your field.

This isn't about fantasy. It's **precision engineering of vibration**.

The body sleeps, but the field listens.

Let it marinate in coherence.

This is how you wake up already ahead of the timeline.

Final Words on Ritual as Reality

A ritual is not a routine. It's not about discipline or perfection. A ritual is a **sacred repetition with energetic intention**. It tells the universe: *This is who I am. Watch me prove it.* It tells your cells: *This is what we're normalizing now.*

When you build a daily alchemy ritual, you stop manifesting in bursts. You start **living in manifestation mode**. Your life becomes the spell. Your energy becomes *automatic calibration.*

And the best part? You don't need hours. You need **consistency with consciousness**.

You don't need more steps. You need **reverence for the steps you already take**.

Drink your coffee like a ceremony. Walk your dog like a priestess. Wash your face like a king. Everything can be sacred when it's done with presence.

This is the path of the embodied creator. Not hustling. Not hoping. But **holding the field**. Every morning. Every moment. Every night.

Because magic doesn't just show up. **You show up—and magic follows**.

Now that your ritual is in place, it's time to stretch reality itself.

Chapter 10: Collapse Time with Timeline Hopping

Most people move through life as if time is linear, slow, and dictated by effort. They believe change takes time, growth takes years, and dreams manifest only if they've "earned it" step by step. That's one way to live. But it's not the only way.

In alchemy, time isn't rigid. It's elastic. It bends to frequency. It obeys the clarity of signal and the depth of embodiment. When you understand this, you stop crawling toward your desired future—and begin hopping into timelines where it's already true.

Timeline Hopping is not science fiction. It's an energetic fact. You're already doing it unconsciously all the time. Every time you make a new choice, take a bold action, or speak a different truth, you shift to a new version of reality. The difference is, most people hop *accidentally*—based on fear, emotion, or default patterns.

But an alchemist does it **intentionally**.

This chapter will teach you how to collapse the perceived delay between "I want it" and "I live it." We'll explore how to sense timelines, align to them, and leap—not with your feet, but with your field.

You're not waiting for your future anymore.

You're *choosing it now*.

Timelines Are Stacked Possibilities, Not Distant Destinations

What we call "the future" is not a fixed point you move toward. It's a **stack of potentials**—parallel timelines layered like sheets of paper, all available now. Each one reflects a different version of you, based on the thoughts you think, the choices you make, the energy you carry, and the identity you claim.

Imagine you're standing at the center of a wheel. Every speech leads to a different timeline. Some are subtle shifts. Others are radical. But all of them are reachable—not by time, but by **tuning**.

The version of you who has the life you want already exists in a vibrational blueprint.

That version is not waiting for you to arrive someday. That version is available right now—as soon as you **match its frequency and make decisions from its state**.

This is where time collapses. Not because you force speed, but because you stop aligning with the version of you that's "getting there someday." You start embodying the one who *is already there.*

That embodiment changes everything.

You begin to notice opportunities that weren't visible before. People treat you differently. Your actions shift. Your confidence rises. The world mirrors the new signal.

And what looked like a five-year journey suddenly becomes a **30-day quantum jump.**

This isn't a delusion. It's energetic geometry.

You're not predicting the future.

You're **selecting** it.

And the moment you stabilize that selection—time bends around it.

Embodiment is the Key to the Jump

Timeline Hopping is not a mental trick. You don't just think yourself into a new reality—you *become* the person who lives in that reality. That's why embodiment is non-negotiable.

You can't collapse time with visualization alone. You must feel, speak, breathe, and behave as if you already live in the timeline you want.

This is what separates wishful thinkers from quantum creators.

Let's say you want to collapse the time it takes to grow your business. You could grind harder and hope something breaks through. Or—you could identify the version of you who already runs a successful business and ask:

- How does she move through her day?

- What does he prioritize, ignore, say no to?

- How does she feel about money, clients, visibility, and risk?

- What does his energy feel like the moment he wakes up?

Then—you copy that blueprint. Not perfectly. But faithfully.

This is not pretending. This is **anchoring to a new identity**. And every time you choose to act from that version of you—even if you're scared—you hop timelines.

You're no longer matching your past.

You're matching your *inevitable self.*

And when that match stabilizes, the outer reality accelerates to catch up.

Here's the catch: your current life may not reflect that new timeline right away. That's okay. The field takes time to organize around new frequencies. Your job isn't to demand instant proof. Your job is to **hold the signal longer than the doubt.**

That's the test. Most people drop the frequency because they don't see fast results. But the ones who collapse time are those who keep choosing the new identity—until the world *has to respond.*

You're not chasing results.

You're **enforcing alignment.**

That's how you leap.

Collapse Points and Identity Triggers

Every timeline hop has a **collapse point**—a moment where the old identity is challenged and the new one must be claimed. It often shows up as discomfort, fear, uncertainty, or a trigger that tempts you to go back to the familiar.

This is the fork in the road. The portal. The test of readiness.

Let's say you're stepping into a wealth timeline. Suddenly, you're hit with an unexpected bill. You could spiral into scarcity, reinforcing the old timeline. Or you could stay rooted in abundance, knowing this moment is a test of signal, not a setback.

When the collapse point hits, don't panic.

Instead, ask:

- What timeline is this moment inviting me into?

- What would my next-level self do here?

- What action affirms the version of me I'm becoming?

The answer is usually bold, uncomfortable, and direct. It's the decision that breaks the cycle.

Because timelines don't shift by comfort.

They shift by **choice in the face of friction**.

Every time you respond differently, you send a shockwave through your field. You tell the universe, *"I'm serious now."* You reinforce the new trajectory.

And when enough of these choices stack? The old reality crumbles. It has no foundation left.

That's the moment you turn around and realize—you're no longer hoping. You're *already there*.

This is why triggers are sacred. They're collapse points in disguise. They show you exactly where you're still loyal to the old self. Not to punish—but to offer the **opportunity to hop**.

Be grateful when life squeezes you.

It means a jump is near.

Final Words on Quantum Leaping

Timeline Hopping isn't fantasy—it's energetic architecture.

It's the discipline of embodying your chosen self *before* the evidence arrives. It's the decision to stop waiting and start creating **from the end**, not toward it.

Most people live in default timelines. Alchemists live in **deliberate ones**.

Here's how to keep leaping:

- **Choose daily**. Every morning, ask: Who am I choosing to be today?

- **Act now**. Take action that affirms your desired timeline—not someday, *now*.

- **Expect tests**. When contrast shows up, lean in. Respond from your future.

- **Celebrate signs**. Every synchronicity, every shift, every subtle change—mark it. You're aligning.

- **Don't wobble**. If you fall off, recalibrate quickly. The timeline doesn't collapse unless *you do*.

You are not waiting for life to approve your next chapter.

You are *initiating it*.

And once you've collapsed time—once you've stabilized the frequency—it's no longer a leap. It's just your *new normal*.

Chapter 11: Shadow Integration for Manifestation Power

Manifestation isn't all light, love, and high vibes. True creation—the kind that rewires your life from the inside out—requires going into the dark. Not to drown in it, but to **reclaim the power you've exiled there**.

Your shadow is not your enemy. It is not something to fix, heal, or avoid. Your shadow is everything you've pushed away: unacknowledged emotions, suppressed desires, unintegrated wounds, unconscious beliefs, disowned brilliance. And it doesn't disappear just because you affirm something else. It waits.

And the longer you avoid it, the more it manipulates your field from the background. It becomes the hidden saboteur of your manifestations—the unseen force pulling you back into old patterns, unworthy timelines, and emotional loops that don't reflect your conscious desires.

If you keep manifesting misalignment, chances are your shadow is running the show.

This chapter isn't about fixing your shadow. It's about **integrating it**. Bringing it into the light of your awareness and turning it into raw, usable power. Because when your shadow and your light work together, you become **unshakable**.

No more self-sabotage. No more pretending. Just full-spectrum embodiment.

Let's bring the whole of you online—so your energy becomes undeniable.

What Is the Shadow?

Carl Jung said, "The shadow is everything about ourselves we do not know." But let's go deeper. In alchemical terms, your shadow is your **unclaimed gold**. It is made up of every part of you that your ego labeled unworthy, dangerous, too much, too emotional, too needy, too powerful—and shoved into the basement.

But here's the truth: nothing in your shadow is inherently bad. It's simply **unintegrated**. And what you refuse to integrate will always control you from the dark.

Your shadow can include:

- The fear you've never let yourself feel

- The ambition you've been taught to suppress

- The rage that boils under your "niceness"

- The jealousy that points to unmet desire

- The guilt that hides behind your productivity

- The worth you abandoned to be loved

And the most dangerous shadows? The ones you don't even know are there. The ones you've spiritualized away. The ones that wear masks like "I'm fine," "I've forgiven," or "I already healed that."

Those shadows whisper behind every manifestation:

"I'm not safe being seen."

"I'll be rejected if I shine."

"Love always leaves."

"Money only comes through struggle."

They aren't evil. They're scared. They were created to protect you. But protection becomes a prison when the threat is long gone.

So we must meet these parts—not with shame, but with **curiosity and courage**.

The alchemist doesn't bypass the shadow. They **mine it**.

Because in that darkness is where your most potent gold is hiding.

Signs Your Shadow Is Blocking Your Manifestation

Shadow blocks are sneaky. They don't usually shout. They slip in through feelings, patterns, and recurring themes in your life that don't match your intentions.

Here's how to spot a shadow playing out:

1. **You keep sabotaging good things**

You launch the offer, then ghost your audience. You meet someone amazing, then pick a fight. You get the opportunity, then freeze. That's not failure. That's a part of you that doesn't feel safe **receiving**. Your shadow might associate success with abandonment, visibility with danger, or abundance with rejection.

2.   **You repeat emotional loops.**

You keep manifesting the same kind of partner. The same scarcity pattern. The same power struggle. Even when the people change, the *feeling* stays the same. That's a shadow script playing on loop. It will keep attracting mirrors until you rewrite it.

3.   **You have strong emotional reactions that feel bigger than the moment.**

Ever been irrationally triggered by someone else's success? Or panicked over a small rejection? That intensity is a clue. It means the situation touched a shadow wound—something deeper, older, unresolved.

4.   **You feel stuck between knowing and doing.**

You've done the courses. You know the concepts. But your results don't reflect your knowledge. That's often a sign that an unconscious belief or identity is pulling you back into an outdated vibration.

Once you spot these patterns, the work begins. But it's not about "fixing" them. It's about listening to the part of you behind them.

The shadow doesn't need to be fixed. It needs to be **witnessed**.

Only then can it let go of its grip on your manifestations.

How to Integrate the Shadow and Reclaim Your Power

Shadow integration isn't a one-time event. It's an ongoing conversation with your unconscious. But once you open that dialogue, you stop leaking energy. You stop resisting your own power. You stop running from what you don't want to feel.

Integration is the act of making the shadow **conscious, honored, and useful**.

Here's how to start:

1.   **Name the Hidden Part**

When something triggers you, instead of reacting, pause. Ask: *What part of me is being activated? What belief, fear, or wound is surfacing?*

Then give it a name. "Ah, this is the part of me that believes I'm not lovable if I'm too successful." "This is the version of me that learned to shrink to feel safe."

Naming brings it into awareness. It creates **separation from identification**.

2.   **Dialogue With Compassion**

Once identified, don't push the shadow away. Don't try to replace it with a "better thought." That's spiritual bypassing. Instead, get curious.

Ask:

- *Why are you here?*

- *What are you trying to protect me from?*

- *What do you need to feel safe releasing this role?*

Often the shadow is a younger version of you. A child who learned to survive by dimming, pleasing, or hiding. When you approach it with love, not judgment, it begins to trust you. And trust opens the door to transformation.

3.   **Integrate Through Expression**

The shadow lives in the body. It must be moved, expressed, and released. Not just intellectualized.

That might mean:

- **Voice work**: Speaking the unsaid truth out loud in a safe space

- **Somatic release**: Moving the emotion through dance, breath, shaking

- **Rage rituals**: Screaming into a pillow, hitting the bed with a towel, releasing anger with intention

- **Writing**: Letting the shadow write a letter, a confession, a declaration

These aren't dramatic—they're **clearing mechanisms**. They unhook the emotional charge from the shadow belief and make space for a new identity to emerge.

When you express the shadow safely, it **alchemizes into clarity**.

4.   **Choose a New Integration Identity**

Once the charge is released, you have a choice: Who do I become now that I no longer need that protection?

This is where manifestation power returns.

You choose the integrated version of you—confident, magnetic, whole—and begin **living from that signal**. You don't deny the past. You just stop letting it drive.

That's shadow transmutation.

It's not about pretending to be someone else.

It's about *reclaiming all of you*—especially the parts you left behind.

Final Words on Becoming Whole

You can't manifest fully if you're rejecting parts of yourself.
 You can't hold abundance if half of you still believe you're unworthy.
 You can't leap timelines if your shadow is clinging to safety.

But when you integrate, when you face what you once avoided, something wild happens:

You become whole.

And wholeness is magnetic.

People feel it. Opportunities feel it. The field feels it. Because your signal is no longer fractured. It's coherent, grounded, and complete.

You stop chasing what you want and start **receiving what matches your integration**.

This is the secret most spiritual creators avoid. They stay in the light and wonder why things don't stick. But the alchemist knows:

You don't get what you *want*.

You get what you are **willing to embody—in totality**.

Light and dark.

Power and pain.

Gold and grit.

You.

Chapter 12: The Signature Vibration Formula

By now, you've understood that manifestation isn't about chasing things. It's about **becoming a field that draws things in**. But here's the deeper layer: you're not here to just be *magnetic*. You're here to be *precisely magnetic*—to emit a signal so uniquely you, so consistent, that what you attract is not just random "good stuff" but the exact experiences, people, and opportunities that fit your blueprint like a lock to a key.

That's your **signature vibration**. Think of it as your energetic fingerprint—an encoded frequency that carries your essence, your power, your purpose, your truth. It's not something you have to invent. It's already within you. But it *does* need to be remembered, refined, and stabilized.

Most people send mixed signals to the universe. They feel powerful one moment, and doubtful the next. They say they want success but carry shame around being seen. They crave abundance but act from fear. That inconsistency creates static. The field doesn't respond to what you say—it responds to **what you consistently broadcast**.

This chapter is about helping you identify, embody, and stabilize your **core frequency**—so that everything you do, say, create, and attract comes from that vibration. No more scrambling to match others. No more trying to "get it right." Just full-spectrum, unapologetic *you*—on frequency, all the time.

That's when manifestation becomes effortless. Because you're no longer signaling confusion. You're *radiating coherence*.

Discovering Your Core Frequency Ingredients

Every signature vibration is made of components. It's not a single word or concept—it's a **composition**, a recipe of energies that make up your essence. To discover your formula, we have to unpack the emotional and energetic codes that live under your desires, your gifts, your patterns, and your impact.

Start by answering these core prompts—not intellectually, but intuitively:

1.   What emotions feel most like "home" to you?

Not comfort zones, but **your truth**. This could be peace, clarity, sovereignty, depth, devotion, boldness, serenity, fire, elegance, wildness. These are clues.

2.   What kind of energy do people consistently receive from you—without you trying?

Maybe it's grounded calm. Maybe it's visionary fire. Maybe it's heart-opening safety. Ask people close to you. Look at testimonials. Notice patterns. These are **transmission traits**—part of your field.

3.   What version of you feels most natural, alive, and free?

Not the role you play. Not the performer. The *real you*. Who is she/he/they? How do they move, speak, and feel?

4.   What do you *not* want to radiate anymore?

Some of your current frequency may be residue: people-pleasing, scarcity, anxiety, overthinking. Identify what's no longer welcome in your field. Purge it.

From these prompts, start collecting **keywords and energies**. You'll notice 3–5 recurring themes. That's your **core vibration stack**.

Let's say your formula is: **Bold + Sacred + Clear + Open**.

That means your unique field is about *leading with courage, holding space with reverence, speaking truth with precision, and receiving with softness*. When you operate from that stack, the field says: "Ah, she's on. Let's deliver her aligned results."

This is not just an identity. It's an *instruction set* for the universe.

The more you clarify it, the more life responds.

Encoding Your Frequency into Thoughts, Words, and Actions

Once you've identified your formula, the next step is to **code it into everything you do**. The mistake most people make is thinking that knowing their frequency is enough. It's not. The field responds to **expression, not intention**.

Let's break down how to start encoding your frequency into your daily experience.

1.   **Thoughts**

Your internal dialogue is the first place to practice. When you catch yourself thinking from a frequency that doesn't match your formula (for example, self-doubt if your formula includes "sovereignty"), pause and redirect.

Ask: *Is this thought aligned with my signature vibration?*

Then reframe: *How would Bold + Sacred + Clear + Open think about this situation?*

This isn't fake positivity. It's **energetic congruence training**.

2.   **Words**

Your spoken and written language should reflect your core frequency. If your vibration includes "elegance," but your language is sloppy or apologetic, you're sending mixed signals.

Refine your tone. Own your voice. Speak with the energy of your chosen formula.

In sales, content, and conversations—let your field speak first, your words follow.

People don't buy your product. They buy your **frequency**.

3.   **Actions**

Every choice you make is a vote for a timeline. Before acting, pause and ask: *Is this action aligned with my signature vibration—or am I betraying it to be accepted or safe?*

Aligned action feels both powerful and peaceful. It might stretch you—but it will never contort you.

When your decisions, boundaries, habits, and rhythms come from your encoded field, you become **energetically trustworthy**—to yourself and the universe.

The result? Less resistance. More synchronicity. Because the field loves **coherence**.

You're not just wishing for a new life.

You're broadcasting it in HD.

Stabilizing the Signal: Rituals, Anchors, and Maintenance

Having a formula is powerful. Embodying it is magnetic. But the real mastery? **Maintaining it when life shakes you**.

Stabilizing your signature frequency is like tending a sacred flame. You don't need to obsess—but you do need to be intentional.

72

Here's how to keep your signal clean, consistent, and strong.

1. **Daily Calibration Rituals**

Build in simple, repeatable practices that reconnect you to your formula.

- Morning mantra: Speak your formula out loud before doing anything else.

- Signature movement: Move your body in a way that expresses your frequency—slow and grounded, or sharp and powerful.

- Anchor object: Wear or carry something that holds the energy of your formula. Touch it when you feel off-center.

These small acts build **energetic memory** in your system.

2. **Environmental Alignment**

Your space affects your frequency. Design your environment to reflect your core vibration. If your formula includes "clarity," declutter your desk. If it includes "sacred," light a candle. If it includes "fire," surround yourself with bold colors or music.

Your physical space should **amplify your chosen field**, not dilute it.

3. **Frequency Check-Ins**

Once a week, review your alignment.

Ask:

- Did I live from my signature this week?

- Where did I wobble? Why?

- Where did I overperform or underplay?

- What helped me stay anchored?

This reflection isn't punishment. It's power. It keeps your formula **active, alive, and evolving**.

Remember: your frequency will evolve as you expand. Don't rigidly cling to words or concepts. Keep listening. Keep refining.

Your signature vibration is not a brand. It's your **energetic DNA made conscious**. And when you live from it, everything aligns.

You attract partners, clients, ideas, and timelines that resonate. You repel misalignment naturally. You become a walking transmission of your truth.

You no longer chase.

You **transmit**.

You are no longer convinced.

You **radiate**.

And that's when manifestation becomes effortless—because it's no longer about getting anything. It's about **being exactly who you came here to be**.

PART IV: MATERIALIZATION METHODS

Chapter 13: Encoded Action: How to Move Energetically, Not Just Physically

You've probably heard the phrase "take aligned action" a hundred times. But let's be honest—most people don't know what that means. They confuse it with productivity. Hustle. Getting things done. They think manifestation is about *doing more, doing it faster,* or *doing it better.*

But in alchemy, **not all action is equal**.

You can do all the "right things" and still repel what you want if the frequency behind your action is misaligned. Because the universe doesn't respond to motion—it responds to **the energy that codes your motion**.

This chapter is about taking **Encoded Action**—the kind that carries your signature vibration aligns with your desired timeline, and creates quantum impact. It's not just about *what* you do. It's about *who* you are while you do it.

When your actions are encoded with clarity, power, truth, and trust, you collapse resistance. You open doors faster. You stop wasting energy chasing things that were never meant for you. You become an intentional transmitter of outcomes.

Let's explore what that looks like in real life—no fluff, no guessing, just pure precision.

Why Most Action Is Just Energetic Static

Let's start with the hard truth: most people are taking frantic, misaligned, low-frequency action. Not because they're lazy, but because they're **unconscious** of what energy they're broadcasting when they move.

For example:

- You launch a new offer but secretly believe no one will buy it.

- You write content that sounds "safe" instead of true, hoping to please everyone.

- You decide for fear—rushing because you're scared of missing out.

That's action, yes—but it's not **encoded**. It's reactive, wobbly, and often coded with

78

desperation, doubt, or unworthiness.

And here's the key: the universe listens to **your energetic instructions**, not your to-do list.

You can't manipulate your way into manifestation. You must **broadcast from embodiment**.

So the first step in encoded action is **awareness**. Before doing anything, pause and ask: *What frequency is this action carrying? Is this signal clear or confused? Am I moving from power, or panic?*

Every action leaves a trace in the field. A footprint. A message.

When it's coded with confidence, congruence, and clarity—life responds fast.

But when it's full of static? You just run in circles.

Encoded action is about breaking that loop.

Calibrating the Field Before the Move

Before you send the email, launch the offer, make the call, and write the post—*calibrate*.

Think of it like charging a spell before casting it. The action is the vessel. But it's **your vibration** that gives it power.

So how do you charge your action?

1.   **Connect to your signature vibration.**

Remember Chapter 12? Before moving, drop into your unique field. Repeat your vibration words. Feel them in your body. Embody them as if they're truth—because they are. You're not doing something *to get* a result. You're doing something *as the version of you who already has it*.

2.   **Anchor into the desired timeline**

Ask: *Which version of me am I acting from right now?* The past self who doubts, or the future self who leads?

Close your eyes. Breathe. Step into the timeline where the action has already worked. Feel what that version of you knows. Then act from *that place*.

This isn't make-believe. It's quantum clarity.

3.   **Choose the encoded intention.**

Infuse the action with a clear intention. Not an attachment. Not "I hope this goes viral" or "I hope this makes money." But: "This post is coded with clarity." "This offer is an energetic match to my field." "This message is a gift, not a grab."

Clean intention creates a magnetic pull.

Now, when you move, you're not just "doing things." You're **casting coded frequencies into the field**.

And that's when momentum becomes *inevitable*.

Action as Identity Rehearsal

The deepest reason to take encoded action is not to get something—it's to **practice being someone**.

Every action you take is a rehearsal of identity. It either reinforces your past or stabilizes your future.

This is why alchemists move differently. They don't act out of obligation or approval-seeking. They act in alignment with their chosen self.

So instead of asking, "What should I do?"

Ask: *What would my expanded self do here—and how do I embody that now?*

For example:

●   The old self-posts online and over-explains, hoping people "get it."
The encoded self-posts once, clearly, powerfully, and lets the field respond.

●   The old self launches only when they feel ready and perfect.
The encoded self launches because they trust their energy speaks louder than their ego.

●   The old self asks questions from lack.
The encoded self asks with curiosity, not fear, and trusts the answer is on its way.

This is where real momentum lives—not in more hustle, but in**congruent identity coding through daily choices**.

And over time, this consistency of character reshapes your field.

You become the person you once visualized.

Not because you said the affirmations. But because you *acted like it*—over and over until the quantum snapped to match.

That's embodiment. That's energetic authorship.

That's an encoded action.

Final Words on Becoming a Living Transmission

You're not here to follow a script. You're here to become **the signal**. A walking, talking, breathing field of encoded frequency.

Every movement you make can be a broadcast. A spell. A declaration.

This means:

- Every button you click carries energy.

- Every word you type sends a signal.

- Every boundary you hold shifts your field.

- Every act of rest, creativity, leadership, visibility—it all *codes the quantum*.

You are always broadcasting.

The question is: are you doing it **intentionally**?

You don't have to "do more." You have to **do less with more alignment**.

Stop performing. Start transmitting.

Stop scrambling. Start commanding.

Stop overthinking. Start coding.

The more intentional your action becomes, the more precise the field gets. The more the universe can read your signal—and deliver on it.

This is how you build momentum that doesn't require burnout.

This is how you manifest without micromanaging.

This is how you shift from effort to inevitability.

Encoded action is not a productivity hack. It's a *power channel*.

Use it wisely.

Chapter 14: The Magnetic Field of Prosperity

You don't attract prosperity by chasing it. You attract prosperity by *becoming the field* where prosperity naturally wants to land.

Most people never realize this. They believe money, wealth, and abundance live "out there"—behind some goal, inside some business, locked behind the effort and hard-earned worthiness. So they hustle. They visualize. They try to be positive about money while internally carrying shame, fear, or resentment around it.

That's why nothing sticks. Because money doesn't respond to what you want. It responds to what you are a **match for**.

In energetic alchemy, abundance is not something you earn. It's a **frequency you stabilize**. And once you do, that field becomes magnetic—not only to money, but to opportunities, support, upgrades, and experiences that reflect expansion.

This chapter will show you how to build your **magnetic field of prosperity** from the inside out. You'll learn to detach from performative "high vibes," reclaim your worth without conditions, and create a reality where receiving becomes natural—because your energy makes it *inevitable*.

This isn't about theory. It's about **frequency sovereignty**. You decide what your field allows, holds, and multiplies.

Let's rewire prosperity at the level that matters: the field behind everything.

Your Frequency Is the Wallet

We've been trained to think money lives in banks, systems, platforms, or clients. But here's the truth: your actual wallet is **your field**.

Your frequency is what determines how money flows, how it stays, and how it multiplies. If your energy is full of fear, guilt, and unworthiness, it doesn't matter how many strategies you use. You might attract money, but you'll also repel it. You'll spend it unconsciously, underprice yourself, or sabotage your flow.

This is why the wealthy are not always the most skilled or the hardest working—they are often simply the most **coherent with receiving**.

So before you try to "make more money," ask: *Can I hold more money? Can I stabilize the frequency of abundance, even without external proof?*

Here's how scarcity usually shows up in your field:

- You feel tension when checking your bank account

- You undercharge or over-give to be liked

- You spend impulsively, then feel guilt

- You say yes to clients, jobs, or tasks that feel misaligned

- You delay decisions out of fear of "what if it runs out?"

These patterns are not about the money—they're about your **energetic relationship** with prosperity. They tell the field: "I don't feel safe with abundance. I don't trust it will stay. I don't believe I'm allowed to receive freely."

To change the flow, you must **change the field**.

This starts by realizing that *you are the source. Not the client. Not the job. Not the sale. Your energy is the faucet. Everything else is plumbing.*

From this perspective, prosperity becomes an inside job.

Your frequency *is* the currency.

And the cleaner it is, the more naturally wealth flows in and stays.

Wealth Codes: Beliefs That Expand or Contract the Field

Your magnetic field is shaped by the codes you carry. These are subconscious beliefs, stories, and emotional imprints that either open the gates to prosperity or block it.

Let's look at the most common **contractive codes** that repel abundance:

- "I have to work hard to deserve money."

- "If I receive too much, others will judge me."

- "I'll lose love if I become wealthy."

- "I'm only valuable when I'm producing."

- "Money is unstable, so I must control everything."

These codes may seem subtle, but they run deep. And they generate a field of scarcity, lack, over-efforting, and exhaustion.

To rewrite them, you must bring them into the light—not to shame them, but to *transmute* them.

Ask yourself:

- What did I learn about money growing up?

- Who did I have to become to feel financially safe?

- What do I believe I have to do to be "allowed" to receive?

- What parts of me feel unsafe with overflow?

These questions expose the energetic roots. Once exposed, you can choose new **expansive wealth codes**, such as:

- "My receiving is a service to the collective."

- "The more I rest, the more I open to overflow."

- "Money follows my clarity, not my effort."

- "Prosperity is safe, stable, and sacred in my hands."

- "I am worthy of wealth simply because I exist."

These new codes must be **felt, spoken, and stabilized**. They aren't affirmations you repeat once. They're frequencies you practice daily—especially when scarcity tries to creep back in.

The moment you hold these new beliefs *even when your circumstances haven't changed*, you collapse old timelines and open portals to wealth.

Your field shifts.

And wealth starts to treat you differently.

Embodying Prosperity Before It Arrives

Here's the master key: the field doesn't shift when you receive money. The field shifts when you **become the version of you who holds prosperity—before the money arrives**.

This is where most people wobble. They wait to feel rich until the bank account confirms it. But in alchemy, manifestation requires the opposite: *You lead with the energy, and the physical follows.*

So how do you embody prosperity in the now?

1.   **Calibrate Your Nervous System to Safety**

 If abundance feels overwhelming or unsafe, your body will reject it—no matter what you say mentally.

Practice regulating yourself with breath, presence, and awareness. When you think about receiving more, tune into your body. Are you tense? Bracing? Spinning? If so, pause. Breathe. Repeat: *I am safe to receive.* This tells your body: "We can hold more. We won't die if we grow."

2.   **Make Decisions Like the Prosperous Version of You**

 Every decision is a code. Ask: *What would the wealthy version of me do here—not recklessly, but with calm clarity?*

Maybe she invests in support. Maybe he says no to scarcity clients. Maybe they rest even when there's pressure to grind.

Move from that place—not just once, but daily.

This stabilizes the version of you who holds wealth with ease.

3.   **Celebrate Without Proof**

 Don't wait for external wins to feel worthy. Train your field to celebrate alignment, not the outcome.

Celebrate when you say no to self-worth. When you price your offer with honesty. When you hold your boundaries. When you choose rest over panic.

These are **prosperity behaviors**. They build a new field.

And eventually, the money catches up.

Not because you chased it, but because your energy called it in like gravity.

This is the magnetic field of prosperity. Not a goal, not a finish line, but a *way of being*.

Final Words on Abundance as Atmosphere

You are not here to earn your right to receive. You're here to remember it.

You are not here to fight scarcity. You're here to **outgrow it energetically**.

Abundance is not a reward. It's a resonance.

And once you hold that resonance—through your thoughts, your choices, your nervous system, your self-trust—the field reorganizes around it. Clients appear. Sales flow. Support arrives. Resources multiply.

Not because you begged.

But because you *became the frequency that couldn't be ignored.*

This is what it means to live inside the magnetic field of prosperity.

It's not always visible at first. But once you hold the signal consistently, the outer world can't help but bow to it.

You're no longer chasing wealth.

You *are* wealth—in motion, in stillness, in breath.

Chapter 15: Sacred Symbols & Manifestation Anchors

We live in a symbolic universe. Every structure, letter, image, and pattern carries meaning—and more importantly, it carries frequency. In ancient alchemy and esoteric traditions, symbols weren't decoration. They were technology. Compressed codes of intent, energy, and archetype.

When used correctly, symbols don't just *represent* power—they **transmit** it.

This chapter is about using sacred symbols and manifestation anchors to **stabilize your energetic field**, magnify intention, and embed desire into the quantum with precision. You've already learned how to encode your thoughts, actions, and identity. Now we give the field **a visual language** that can mirror, amplify, and reflect as form.

Manifestation isn't only about feeling. It's about anchoring. And nothing anchors subtle energy like a **symbol coded with intention**.

Whether it's a hand-drawn sigil, a grid under your pillow, or a glyph etched into your phone background, these tools become *fixed points in the quantum*—places where your field can return, stabilize, and expand.

It's time to build your **visual technology of creation**.

The Power of Symbolic Compression

A symbol is a container. It holds complexity in simplicity. One shape can contain pages of intention. That's why they're so powerful—they bypass the logical mind and speak directly to the subconscious and the field.

Think of a symbol like a folder on a computer. You click it, and it opens an entire program. Sacred symbols work the same way—they store the frequency of your desire and allow you to access it instantly.

This is especially useful when your energy wobbles. When you're overwhelmed, unsure, or drifting out of alignment, a symbol can **recall your frequency** faster than words. It becomes a stabilizer, a reminder, and a beacon.

The ancients knew this. Cultures across time used symbols to invoke gods, anchor spells, direct energy, and protect space. Egyptians had hieroglyphs. Celts had spirals. Indigenous people carved spirit codes into earth and wood. None of this was aesthetic. It was **functional alchemy**.

Now, you get to do the same.

You don't need a priesthood or permission. You just need **intention + attention + form**.

Start by asking: *What do I want this symbol to encode?*

Clarity is key. Symbols work best when created for a **specific field effect**—such as:

- Attracting aligned clients

- Protecting your energy

- Holding abundance

- Strengthening your timeline

- Remembering your essence

- Opening the heart

Once you define the intent, the form begins to emerge.

Whether you draw it yourself or select from existing symbols, the energy behind it is what activates the power.

Because symbols are not magic.

Your belief + focus + consistency is the magic.

The symbol is just a transmitter.

Creating Your Sigil

Sigils are one of the most accessible forms of manifestation symbols. They're visual representations of desire, shaped into abstract symbols that bypass the rational brain and go straight into the subconscious.

Creating one is simple—but don't mistake that simplicity for weakness. When crafted and charged correctly, a sigil becomes a **living spell**—an anchor for your intent in physical form.

Here's how to create one:

1.   **Clarify Your Intent**

Write a present-tense statement that reflects your desired reality. Not "I want to attract aligned clients," but "I attract aligned clients with ease and joy." Keep it simple, clear, and affirmative.

2.   **Distill the Letters**

Remove all repeating letters. This reduces the sentence to its energetic essence. For example, "I attract aligned clients with ease and joy" becomes "IATRCLNDSEJWY."

3.   **Turn Letters into Design**

Take those letters and begin crafting them into a symbol. You can combine, stack, or morph them into an abstract glyph. It doesn't need to be legible. The less recognizable it is, the better it bypasses your logical mind.

4.   **Charge the Sigil**

The sigil needs energy to activate. This is where intention becomes alchemical. Charge it by focusing on it during peak emotional states—after breathwork, dance, meditation, sex, or even laughter. Imprint the symbol with the frequency of belief.

5.   **Release and Anchor**

You can burn the paper, hide it, wear it, place it under your pillow, make it your phone background—whatever feels aligned. The point is: to release it into the field while trusting the work is done.

Your sigil now becomes a **frequency transmitter**. Not loud, not frantic—just quietly, powerfully pulsing your intent into the quantum every time you see it or pass by it.

Over time, your subconscious will begin to match the symbol's energy. The external world will respond.

You've just created visual magic—and it's working whether you think about it or not.

Using Grids, Glyphs, and Physical Anchors

While sigils are personal and portable, grids and physical anchors bring another layer of potency: **structure + stability.**

Energy loves structure. And when you place intention within a sacred arrangement, it amplifies. It creates a container that holds, radiates, and refines your field.

Let's look at three ways to do this:

1.   **Crystal Grids**

You don't have to be a crystal expert. Choose stones that resonate with your intent (citrine for abundance, rose quartz for love, obsidian for protection), and place them in a geometric pattern on a table, altar, or under your bed. Add your sigil in the center if you like.

Each crystal becomes a node. The layout becomes a **network of frequencies** that echo your desire across time and space.

Keep the grid charged by placing your hands over it daily and breathing your intent into it. It becomes a silent worker—anchoring your manifestation in the background.

2.   **Glyph Tattoos or Wearables**

Some frequencies deserve to be part of your body. Consider designing a symbolic glyph—your essence in visual form—and etching it onto your skin (permanently or temporarily), or wearing it as jewelry.

These are not fashion statements. They are **identity activators**. Every time you see or feel the symbol, your body remembers the field it belongs to.

This creates cellular congruence—manifestation from the inside out.

3.   **Physical Anchors in Space**

Place your symbol somewhere visible: your mirror, desk, wallet, or altar. These visual cues become **energetic checkpoints**. Every time you see them, take a breath and drop into the frequency they represent.

They're like bookmarks for your field—reminding you who you are and what you're creating.

You can even code objects intentionally. That ring you wear? Charge it with the frequency of visibility. That pen you write with? Charge it with the frequency of flow. That cup you drink from each morning? Imbue it with self-worth.

In the alchemist's world, **everything is a portal**—if you let it be.

Final Words on Visual Alchemy

You've been taught that symbols are passive decorations. But they're not. They're **active field tools**, capable of holding, amplifying, and transmitting intent across dimensions.

When you work with symbols, you give your energy a body.

When you create sigils, grids, or glyphs, you stop hoping and start anchoring.

You give the quantum something to grip, to echo, to match.

Your manifestation becomes **geometric**—not just emotional.

As you keep your field clear, your attention consistent, and your symbols charged, the gap between thought and form begins to close.

You're no longer casting spells with your words alone.

You're sculpting reality with image, shape, and form.

This is a manifestation beyond vision boards. This is **energetic engineering**.

Chapter 16: Co-Creating with the Quantum Field

Up until now, we've explored how to shape energy through identity, emotion, frequency, and form. You've learned how to become the architect of your reality, how to stabilize a magnetic field, and how to encode action that reverberates across timelines.

But here's a deeper truth: you're not manifesting in a vacuum. You're not the only force at play.

You are not the Source—you are a sovereign *extension* of it. And the field you're transmitting into? It's not just a void waiting for instructions. It's a living, conscious intelligence. It listens. It learns. It responds. And most importantly—it *wants to co-create with you.*

Co-creation is the art of moving with the quantum field—not as a beggar, not as a puppeteer, but as a collaborator. A sacred partner. A force that understands that real power doesn't come from control—it comes from *congruence.*

This chapter is about stepping into a full-spectrum relationship with the invisible intelligence of the field. Because the most powerful manifestations don't come from force—they come from *synergy.*

You're about to learn how to initiate that relationship, recognize its language, and trust its timing.

The ego commands.

The alchemist *converses.*

The Field Is Listening—Are You Speaking Its Language?

The quantum field doesn't speak English, Spanish, or Italian. It doesn't understand spreadsheets or action plans. It doesn't care about your logic or your timelines. What it responds to—*flawlessly*—is frequency.

Frequency is its native tongue. And everything you think, feel, believe, and do is broadcasting that frequency constantly.

But here's the glitch: most people are speaking static.

They say they want abundance, but their bodies pulse fear.

They write down their goals, but their field screams "not ready."

They visualize freedom while embodying contraction.

This is not failure—it's feedback. And the field is always listening.

So the first step in co-creation is to **become fluent in frequency**. That means cleaning your signal, clarifying your intentions, and being brutally honest about what you're transmitting.

Ask yourself daily:

- What am I broadcasting right now?

- Is my energy congruent with what I claim to want?

- What frequency am I inviting the field to mirror?

The clearer your frequency, the faster the response.

The field doesn't need you to work harder. It needs you to get **consistent**.

Once your signal is clean, the next step is learning how the field *talks back*.

Because it does.

But not in words.

In signs, nudges, delays, synchronicities, sudden shifts, intuitive pulls. You won't hear a booming voice say "Turn left"—but you might feel a subtle yes in your gut, or a strange resistance in your chest.

These are not random. They are *responses*. Invitations.

The more you trust them, the more fluent your co-creation becomes.

Releasing the Need to Control Outcomes

The biggest mistake spiritual creators make is thinking they must direct every detail. They try to manifest like control freaks—telling the field exactly how, when, and through whom their results should appear.

But here's the paradox: **the more you control, the less room the field has to deliver something better**.

The quantum field is infinite. It has access to paths, people, and portals you couldn't possibly predict. But when you cling to specifics, you lock yourself into a narrow frequency—and collapse the magic.

Co-creation requires trust.

You set the intention. You hold the frequency. You take the aligned action.

Then you **release the attachment to how it has to arrive**.

This isn't passive. This is *mastery*. Think of it like planting a seed. You don't dig it up every day to see if it's working. You trust the process. You keep watering. You stay in the energy of bloom, even if you don't see petals yet.

Releasing control doesn't mean you stop caring.

It means you stop micromanaging the universe.

The most powerful manifestations often show up in disguise—through unexpected channels, delays that turn into miracles, or what looks like a failure but is redirection. The field knows what you're asking for—even when you don't. So instead of forcing outcomes, become a **vibrational invitation**.

Say: "This or something even better. I trust. I'm ready."

That surrender creates space for the field to move.

And when it does, it moves *fast*.

Recognizing and Responding to Quantum Feedback

The field doesn't operate on a linear clock. It operates on **vibrational resonance**.

That's why some things manifest in hours while others take months. It's not about effort. It's about *alignment + readiness*.

To truly co-create, you must become a master of **quantum feedback**—learning to read the signs, the delays, the shifts, and the synchronicities *as messages*.

Here are the most common forms of field communication:

1.   **Obstacles or Delays**

Not always "blocks." Often, delays are buffers giving you time to recalibrate. Sometimes, the delay is because your field isn't stable enough to hold the manifestation. Sometimes, it's rerouting you to something more aligned.

When things slow down, ask:

- What is this delay teaching me about my signal?

- What version of me is being invited to rise here?

2.   **Synchronicities**

Repeated numbers. Themes. Songs. Animals. Dreams. Random encounters that feel too perfect to be random.

These are confirmations. The field is saying: *Yes. Keep going. You're tuning in.*

But they only mean something if you *act on them*.

3.   **Sudden Shifts or Endings**

Sometimes the field will collapse a situation to make room for what you asked for. You'll lose a client. A job will fall through. A friend will disappear.

This isn't punishment. It's *refinement*.

You said you wanted alignment. The field is clearing anything that doesn't match.

Don't cling. Respond with curiosity. Ask:

- What is this clearing making space for?

- What timeline is now opening?

4.   **Emotional Intensity**

When something huge is about to land, the ego panics. You may feel sudden fear, anxiety, or resistance.

That's not a red flag. That's a **frequency upgrade** in motion.

Breathe. Ground. Don't react. Let the wave pass. You're stretching into a new bandwidth.

The more you learn to read and respond to feedback like this, the faster your co-creation sharpens.

You stop asking "Why isn't it here yet?"

And start asking, "What is this moment calibrating me for?"

That's when you shift from victim to vessel.

From controller to creator.

From hoping to *knowing*.

Final Words on Sacred Partnership

You are not doing this alone.

You never were.

Every desire you carry is not just a selfish want—it's a divine code. A conversation started by the universe through *you*. The question is: will you respond?

When you enter true co-creation, your life becomes art.

You stop begging. You start dancing.

You stop pushing. You start listening.

This is not passive. This is powerful.

This is a relationship with the mystery.

And like all relationships, it's built on **trust, intimacy, and presence**.

You speak through vibration.

The field replies through the form.

Together, you build new worlds.

So now, ask:

- Am I willing to trust what I cannot yet see?

- Am I ready to release control, and make space for something greater?

- Am I willing to be in conversation with the infinite?

If yes—then step forward.

The field is already listening.

PART V: DOCTRINE
EMBODIED

Chapter 17: Living as an Alchemist in a 3D World

Spiritual awakening is exhilarating—until you realize you still have rent to pay, emails to answer, and dishes to wash. You may feel like a multidimensional light-being in the morning… only to get thrown off by traffic, tech issues, or a passive-aggressive client by lunch.

This is the edge most seekers never cross. They chase expansion in retreats, rituals, and journal prompts—but they haven't yet learned how to **live their frequency while navigating the everyday**.

This chapter is about that edge. The one where energy meets form. Where your highest vision must pass through the friction of the real world. And if you can hold your field *there*—in chaos, boredom, noise, routine—then you don't just "practice" alchemy. You **embody it.**

Living as an alchemist doesn't mean escaping the matrix. It means **operating with sovereignty inside it**.

You don't have to move to a mountaintop or delete Instagram. You just need to become *unshakably aligned* in the middle of real life.

Because manifestation isn't what happens in the ceremony.
It's what happens when your landlord raises the rent—and you stay in frequency.
It's what happens when the launch flops—and you recalibrate without collapsing.
It's how you show up when no one's watching—and you still act as the future self anyway.

That's the real work. That's where magic gets bones and breath and body.

Let's build it.

Holding Frequency in Friction

You've done the visualizations. You've felt the future. But can you **hold the frequency** when your 3D circumstances don't reflect it yet?

This is the part where most people break the spell.

They feel abundant in meditation... but collapse into lack when an unexpected bill hits.

They embody self-worth in affirmations... but shrink when someone doesn't validate them.

They move with power on paper... but hesitate when it's time to post, launch, ask, or lead.

This isn't a failure—it's an invitation. The 3D world isn't here to block you. It's here to **test, refine, and fortify your embodiment**.

Every moment of friction is a chance to stabilize the signal. Not to perform perfection—but to return to resonance. To breathe into the discomfort. To remind your nervous system: *I am safe even here.*

Try this:

- When tension hits, name the frequency you want to return to. (Example: clarity, trust, power)

- Breathe into your body. Find where that frequency lives. Feel it for 60 seconds.

- Ask yourself: *How would I move right now if I truly embodied that frequency?*

Then act from *that* place—not reaction, not panic. Power.

That's what living alchemy looks like. It's not flawless—it's fluid. It doesn't resist the storm. It becomes the eye inside it.

Because in the field, how you respond **is the spell**.

Making the Mundane Sacred

It's easy to feel mystical when the incense is burning and the playlist is vibing. But real power comes from making the ordinary **ritualized**—from seeing *everything* as part of the manifestation process.

That's the shift from fantasy to integration.

Your morning coffee? It's not just caffeine—it's a chance to anchor your day's frequency.
Your Zoom call? Not just work—it's an opportunity to transmit your signature field.
Your walk to the store? Not just movement—it's a ceremony of presence.

When you start seeing your life as a living altar, manifestation accelerates. Because you're no longer compartmentalizing your power. You're **weaving magic into motion**.

Here's how to infuse the mundane with alchemical awareness:

1.   **Assign Meaning to Your Movements**

Before a task, name the frequency you want it to carry. Washing dishes? Presence. Writing emails? Clarity. Cooking dinner? Nourishment. Every action becomes a coded broadcast.

2.   **Use Repetition as Frequency Training**

Most people resent repetition. But alchemists use it to build mastery. Your routines aren't boring—they're opportunities to stabilize your signal. To walk as the future self over and over until it becomes default.

3.   **Create Micro-Rituals**

You don't need hours of the ceremony. A 10-second hand over your heart. A whispered mantra before opening your laptop. A breath before checking your phone. These tiny rituals **stack power**. They remind the field who you are.

When you approach life like this, everything becomes part of the work. Nothing is neutral. Everything is alive.

And the more you treat the mundane with reverence, the more it begins to **respond with miracles**.

Because the field reflects your relationship with *all* of life—not just the shiny parts.

Navigating Relationships Without Losing Your Field

Let's be honest: it's easy to hold frequency when you're alone. But what happens when you're around people who don't "get" what you're doing?

When your partner doubts the path...

When your family rolls their eyes at your magic...

When your friends still live in loops of lack, gossip, and drama...

Do you shrink to fit in? Or can you stay expanded without needing validation?

Living as an alchemist means learning to navigate **relationships from sovereignty**, not from superiority or shame. It means knowing when to speak when to stay silent, and when to protect your field like it's sacred—because it is.

Here's how to move through that with grace:

1. **Release the Need to Convert**

You're not here to convince anyone. Your embodiment is your message. Let them feel your shift. Let your reality speak louder than words. Lead by resonance, not resistance.

2. **Protect Your Field, Not Your Ego**

You're allowed to walk away from conversations that collapse your frequency. You're allowed to limit access to your energy. Boundaries aren't blocks—they're **containers for magic**.

3. **Let Duality Exist**

You can love someone and disagree with them. You can hold your truth and stay open. You don't have to exile yourself to feel powerful. Integration doesn't mean agreement—it means *acceptance without absorption*.

The world won't always reflect your frequency. That's okay.

Your job isn't to be understood.

Your job is to **stay in signal long enough for the field to recalibrate around you**.

And it will.

Reality always catches up to embodiment.

Even if the people around you don't.

Final Words on Alchemy in the Everyday

Living as an alchemist is not a title. It's a practice. A choice you make when it's boring, when it's hard when no one's clapping, when nothing's working—*yet*.

It's how you answer the moment when things wobble.

Do you collapse, or recalibrate?

It's how you hold your power when nobody sees the work you're doing inside.

Do you abandon your timeline, or anchor deeper?

It's how you meet reality—not as something to fight, but as something to **transmute**.

This is the highest magic.

Not escaping the world.

But *infusing it with frequency* so that your life becomes the living evidence of your inner truth.

You don't just visualize the new world.

You walk it.

You breathe it.

You become the portal through which it arrives.

Chapter 18: Mastering Patience, Power, and Paradox

There comes a point in every manifestation journey where you've done "everything right." You've tuned your frequency. You've anchored your intention. You've embodied the version of you who already has it. You've held the signal, trusted the field, and released the timeline.

And still—nothing seems to be happening.

This is the point where most people quit. They doubt. They spiral. They collapse their field and scramble for logic. They start to think manifestation doesn't work—or worse, that they did it wrong.

But in alchemy, this phase is sacred. It's not punishment. It's not a delay. It's a **paradox**.

This chapter is about understanding and mastering the mystery of the gap—the space between encoded intention and visible result. It's about holding power when your mind is screaming for proof. It's about cultivating true energetic sovereignty, not because things are moving fast, but because you trust even when they don't.

Real manifestation requires you to be as powerful in stillness as you are in action.
To remain congruent when reality seems off-track.
Remember that the field often reorganizes in silence—because silence is not absence. Silence is *construction*.

This is where you stop being a dabbler and become a real alchemist.
Not because it's easy—but because you *choose coherence over evidence*.

Let's explore how to stand steady inside the paradox.

When Reality Lags but Energy Leads

In the quantum, things shift instantly. In the 3D world, those shifts take time to show up in form. There's a lag—not because the field is broken, but because **density moves slower than light**.

Think of it like sending an email to another continent. The message is sent instantly, but the person reading it may still be asleep. You don't panic and resend it a hundred times. You trust they'll open it when they're ready.

Your intentions are the same. They've been sent. They've been received. The delay is not denial—it's **alignment in motion**.

This lag is where trust is forged. And most people misinterpret it as a failure.

They say: "It's not working," when what's happening is the field is rearranging the people, events, circumstances, and micro-decisions needed to land the desire into their 3D life.

But here's the key: *you must hold the field steady while that happens*. Because if you shift your frequency in the waiting room, you cancel the delivery.

That's why this phase isn't about waiting.

It's about *wielding*.

You're not sitting in a cosmic timeout. You're being tested for **energetic stability**. Can you hold power without results? Can you stay tuned when nothing appears to be changing? Can you love the desire before it arrives?

Because that's what anchors it.

You think nothing's happening.

The field knows what you're becoming.

Patience as Power, Not Passivity

Let's be clear: patience in alchemy is not weakness. It's **high-level power**.

It's not "I'll wait and suffer." It's "I'll stand as the person who already knows." It's not inaction. It's conscious stillness. It's choosing not to chase, not to beg, not to scramble—and instead, to *remain in signal*.

This kind of patience comes from trust, not endurance.

Most people confuse patience with passivity. But true patience is an **active holding of frequency**.

You're still calibrating. Still creating. Still attuning your nervous system to the future. Still being in conversation with the field. You're just not rushing to fill the silence with noise.

Try this: next time you feel nothing is happening, ask yourself—

- What timeline am I standing on right now?

- What would the version of me who knows it's already done feel right now?

- What small act can I do today that honors my belief in the outcome?

It might be taking a walk as the future self. Journaling as if it's already done. Speaking one sentence aloud with conviction. Holding five minutes of silent frequency in your body.

These are not placeholders. They are **threads that pull the result toward you.**

Every time you hold your energy in stillness, the manifestation gains mass. It becomes real—not because you saw it, but because you believed before evidence demanded it.

That's how timelines stabilize. Not with force. With *unchanging frequency.*

And yes, this requires patience.

But not the kind you were taught.

This is patience laced with certainty.

Not waiting. *Knowing.*

Not hoping. *Becoming.*

And in that, the paradox is no longer the enemy. It's the proof you're ascending.

Dancing with the Unknown

There's one universal law that every alchemist must bow to: **you don't get to know the full "how."**

This is not because the universe wants to test you—it's because true creation comes through **collaboration with mystery**. Mystery, by nature, means you're not in control of every detail.

Most people panic when the "how" isn't clear. They freeze. They loop in logic. They delay action until the plan feels perfect.

But the field doesn't need perfect plans. The field needs *clear signals.*

That's why your job is not to map every step—it's to move from knowing.

When the path isn't visible, you move anyway.

When the response hasn't come, you still transmit.

When the outcome isn't guaranteed, you still choose the timeline that holds the desire.

This is how you dance with the unknown. Not by demanding certainty—but by becoming it.

Ask yourself:

- Can I lead without proof?

- Can I show up with devotion, not desperation?

- Can I let the "how" emerge instead of forcing it?

Because paradox is this: the more you trust, the more the field responds.

The more you release, the more you receive.

The more you lead with energy, the more form bends around you.

You don't collapse into the unknown. You **rise to meet it**.

And when you do, the field opens.

Not because you earned it.

But because you finally aligned with it.

Final Words on Stabilizing Through the Gap

You're not here to manifest by force. You're here to *magnetize by coherence*. And coherence doesn't require visible confirmation to hold power.

The most advanced alchemists manifest not by chasing—but by holding the line when everything in the 3D says "give up."

That's not a delusion. That's *energetic mastery*.

So the next time it feels like nothing is happening, remember:

- You're not stuck. You're *stabilizing*.

- You're not failing. You're *forging faith*.

- You're not lost. You're *learning to lead without needing to see.*

This is how you collapse timelines—not by micromanaging the field, but by becoming unshakable in the void.

Patience becomes your wand.

Power becomes your posture.

Paradox becomes the proof that you're creating something **more real than reality**.

Chapter 19: Teaching, Transmitting, and Leading Energetically

At a certain point on the path of alchemical creation, the question shifts from "What can I manifest?" to "What am I *transmitting* just by existing?"

This is the initiation into energetic leadership—not based on status, strategy, or external influence, but on **vibrational presence**.

You've moved through your shadows. You've rewired your thought field. You've collapsed timelines, held paradoxes, and learned to co-create with the quantum. Now you begin to notice: that people don't just listen to what you say—they respond to who you *are*.

That's not ego. That's embodiment.

This chapter isn't about becoming a coach, influencer, or spiritual figure. It's about recognizing that we are *always transmitting*, whether we know it or not. The question is: are you doing it consciously?

Leadership in this context doesn't require a platform. You don't need a microphone or a million followers.

You just need a stable signal. A clear frequency. A deep willingness to let your field **do the work of inspiration, activation, and permission-giving** without needing credit.

You become the message.

And when you become the message, your life itself becomes the teaching.

Let's explore how to lead with energy—without performance, pressure, or pretense.

Presence Over Performance

We've all seen people say the right things but carry a distorted energy. They speak about love while vibrating control. They preach abundance while transmitting scarcity. They claim empowerment while leaking approval-seeking.

Words don't matter if the frequency isn't clean.

Energetic leadership begins with this truth: your field is louder than your mouth.

People feel your energy *before* they hear your message. They sense the coherence—or lack of it—within seconds. It's not conscious, but it's real. That's why the most powerful teachers are often the most grounded, embodied, and subtle. They don't try to convince you. They *emanate* something. And that something invites others to rise.

You can't fake frequency.

This is why the deepest form of leadership is not performance, but **presence**. The ability to stand in your full energetic signature without needing to adjust, impress, or justify.

That presence is magnetic. Not flashy. Not happy. Just *true*.

To cultivate that, ask:

- Where am I performing instead of simply being?

- What version of me do I broadcast in groups, relationships, and business?

- Is my field congruent with my values, or is it curated?

You don't need to be perfect. But you do need to be *aligned*. Not just when it's easy—but especially when it's uncomfortable.

When your field becomes the teacher, you no longer need to push. You just *stand*. And your presence becomes an activation for others to remember their power.

That's leadership through transmission.

And it's rare.

Because most people are still trying to speak what they haven't fully embodied.

But when you *live* it, you don't need to be convinced.

You radiate truth—and truth rearranges reality.

Teaching Without Preaching

One of the most misunderstood aspects of spiritual or energetic leadership is the impulse to teach through instruction—giving advice, offering frameworks, and over-explaining in the name of service.

But the most effective teaching rarely happens in the conscious mind.

It happens when your field carries a frequency strong enough to **disrupt, rewire, and awaken** another person's field without ever needing to say much.

This is energetic transmission.

Think about it. You've probably met someone who made you feel grounded just by being near them. Or someone whose calmness made you breathe deeper. Or someone who said almost nothing, but left you feeling activated for days.

That's not charisma. That's *field coherence*.

When your frequency is clean, stable, and embodied, it **entrains** others. It speaks directly to their nervous system and subconscious mind. It bypasses resistance. It doesn't ask for permission. It simply *invites* them to recalibrate.

And this is where true teaching happens.

It doesn't require a course or a stage.

It requires depth, truth, and energetic clarity.

To begin leading this way, try the following:

- Speak less, signal more. Let your actions, your decisions, and your energy teach.

- Share from lived experience, not recycled concepts. Authenticity is magnetic.

- Offer insight *only* when it's invited. Teaching without consent becomes an intrusion.

Remember, people aren't looking for more information.

They're looking for **mirrors of possibility**. For evidence that another timeline is real. For someone who has walked the path and can now transmit the *frequency* of what's possible.

If you've done the work, you're that person.

You don't need to shout it.

Just *become the living proof*—and the field will echo your signal where it's needed.

Leading Without Leading

Let's break the final illusion: that to lead means to be "ahead" or to be followed.

True energetic leadership is not hierarchical. It doesn't require others to be behind you. It doesn't need admiration. It doesn't seek control.

It's rooted in **self-responsibility + shared expansion**.

You're not leading to be seen. You're leading because your frequency *can't not*.

This is leadership without ego.

It's what happens when you fully own your power, embody your truth, and offer your presence without attachment.

You become a *north star*—not because you're trying to lead others, but because you're unwavering in your alignment.

In this model, leadership is not something you do. It's something you **are**.

It shows up in everyday ways:

- Holding your truth in family dynamics without needing to prove anything.

- Walking away from misaligned opportunities with grace and clarity.

- Staying regulated in chaos, becoming a stabilizing force for others.

- Taking aligned action when others hesitate, simply because you trust your frequency.

This is silent leadership.

It's not about the spotlight. It's about *signal*.

You stop managing perception and start radiating permission.

And the irony is—this kind of leadership often inspires more impact, more trust, and more transformation than anything flashy ever could.

You're not leading for applause.

You're leading because the field *needs* that frequency anchored somewhere.

You're not leading for followers.

You're leading because your embodiment *requires expression*.

You're not leading for validation.

You're leading because you *are the timeline others are praying to remember exists.*

And that's the kind of leadership this world is starving for.

Not more noise. More *signal.*

Not more instruction. More *integration.*

Not more charisma. More *coherence.*

And you're already it.

You've walked the fire.

You've shaped the field.

You've become the container.

Now let others feel what that does—without needing to explain it.

Your life is already the message.

Let it speak.

In the final chapter, we'll bring it all together.

Not as a concept, not as a technique—but as a new identity.

Because the highest level of manifestation is not when you attract something.

It's when you *become* it.

Chapter 20: The Final Alchemy: Becoming the Spell

There is a point in every alchemist's journey when the tools are no longer needed, the rituals dissolve, and the structure gives way to something purer. It's not that you stop manifesting—but that *manifestation becomes you.*

You are no longer the seeker, the student, or the spellcaster.

You are the spell.

You move through the world, not with force or method, but with *essence.* Everything you've learned—frequency, intention, embodiment, energy—no longer lives in your journal or your vision board. It lives in your **walk**, your **voice**, your **choices**, and the **undeniable resonance** of your field.

In this chapter, we seal the doctrine.

Not with another technique. Not with another concept.

But with a **return**—to the place you were always meant to arrive: full identity-level congruence. The place where your internal truth and your external world are no longer two realities fighting each other, but one seamless, unshakable frequency.

You don't have to manifest things anymore.

You manifest *as* the thing.

This is the final alchemy.

Let's finish what you started.

Identity as the Ultimate Technology

You've used desire, thought, emotion, and intention. You've collapsed timelines and encoded rituals. But at the core of it all—beneath the mechanics and mysticism—is a truth too big for technique:

You manifest who you believe you are.

Not what you want. Not what you visualize.

Who. You. Are.

Your identity is the most consistent broadcast in your field. It is the compass by which your actions, expectations, relationships, and results are determined. And it is often the last thing people change.

They set new goals but keep the same self-concept. They create new affirmations but maintain the same inner posture. They do the work—*but still see themselves as someone doing the work*, instead of someone who already is the embodiment.

This is the final transmutation: dissolving the identity of the seeker and stepping fully into the **I Am** of your desired reality.

What does that mean?

It means walking into a room with no need to prove, perform, or persuade—because your field already says it all.

It means making decisions not to get somewhere, but because *that's what someone like you naturally chooses.*

It means releasing the idea of "attracting" and instead remembering that the world is simply *reflecting* who you've already become.

And yes, identity is fluid. But the anchor of your creation must be **stable**.

So who are you now?

Not who you were. Not who you're hoping to become.

But right now—in this chapter—what's the **core frequency** your life is orbiting around?

Because everything else is just a match to that.

If it feels unfamiliar at first, good.

That means you're shifting.

You don't practice your new identity. You *be it*.

Even when it's awkward.

Even when no one gets it yet.

Even when the evidence lags.

Because this identity is not adopted.

It's *remembered.*

And as you remember, the field catches up.

Because it's been waiting for you to finally claim yourself—not as someone manifesting—but as the **living manifestation**.

Living in the Field of "Already Done"

The most powerful shift you can make is from "I hope it's coming" to "It's already done, and I'm just catching up to it."

This is not a delusion. It's energetic alignment with the version of reality that's already created in the quantum.

You've been told to chase the goal. Push. Hustle. Launch. Repeat.

But in the alchemist's world, you don't chase—*you merge.*

You align with the frequency of your outcome so deeply that reality has no choice but to restructure itself around you.

When you walk in the field of "already done," you start making different moves:

- You don't ask, "How do I get it?"

You ask, "What's the next natural step for someone who already lives it?"

- You don't wait for proof to believe.

You believe so completely that the proof shows up to catch up.

- You don't panic when things feel uncertain.

You rest in the certainty of your identity and let the field recalibrate around it.

This creates a feedback loop of power.

You walk as if.

Reality responds.

You anchor deeper.

Results accelerate.

You become the gravitational pull of your desires.

Not by pushing. Not by obsessing.

But by **standing in the timeline as if it's your address**.

And from that place, you don't need to convince anyone—including yourself.

You're not *going to become.*

 You *are.*

And the field knows it.

Because your energy stopped asking.

 It started *transmitting.*

This is the quantum version of faith—not hope with fingers crossed, but *full-body certainty without proof.*

That's what collapses time.

And the moment you choose it, *you're home.*

Becoming the Spell: A Life Beyond Technique

This doctrine began with tools—rituals, codes, symbols, and intention. And they were necessary. They helped you remember your power. They helped you speak to the field. They helped you hold the signal when the noise was too loud.

But the true magician does not cling to the wand.

At some point, you don't need the steps.

You become the spell.

You don't sit down to script a new reality. You *are* the walking script. You don't "do the work" for one hour a day—you *are* the work. You don't wait for activation. You *transmit it just by being present.*

This is the end of seeking. And the beginning of **embodied presence**.

It's the quiet knowing that your timeline is unfolding not because you're chasing it, but because you've become the field it belongs to.

You still move. You still act. You still take aligned steps.

But none of it is trying to *make something happen.*

It's simply the natural expression of a field that already holds it all.

So now, the real question isn't:

- What should I do?

- What should I manifest next?

- What strategy will get me there?

It's:

Who am I becoming, and how can I let my life speak it louder than my words ever could?

Because that version of you is already encoded in the field.

Not a fantasy. Not a someday.

But a frequency.

And now, you've become it.

That's the final alchemy.

Not turning lead into gold.

But turning identity into essence.

Turning practice into presence.

Turning *doing* into *being*.

You no longer manifest.

You **are** the manifestation.

And the world will bend to reflect you—not because you forced it, but because your frequency made it inevitable.

Congratulations, alchemist.

The doctrine is complete.

But your creation?

It's only just begun.

www.ingramcontent.com/pod-product-compliance
Lightning Source LLC
Chambersburg PA
CBHW070927270326
41927CB00011B/2756